Weary And Ill At Ease

To the clergy and musicians of the Church of England

Seated one day at the organ,
I was weary and ill at ease,
And my fingers wandered idly
Over the noisy keys.

From *The Lost Chord* by Adelaide Procter
set to music by Arthur Sullivan

Weary And Ill At Ease

A Survey Of Clergy And Organists

ROBIN L.D. REES

Gracewing.

First published in 1993

Gracewing
Fowler Wright Books
Southern Ave, Leominster
Herefordshire HR6 0QF

Gracewing Books are distributed

In New Zealand by
Catholic Supplies Ltd
80 Adelaide Road
Wellington
New Zealand

In Australia by
Charles Paine Pty
8 Ferris Street
North Parramatta
NSW 2151 Australia

In USA by
Morehouse Publishing
P.O. Box 1321
Harrisburg
PA 17105
U.S.A.

Typesetting by Robin L.D. Rees

Printed by The Cromwell Press,
Broughton Gifford, Melksham, Wiltshire SN12 8PH

ISBN 085244 231 9

Contents

Foreword

by the Bishop of Oxford

I have always rather prided myself on establishing good relationships with organists and choirmasters. This is rooted in a strong sense of my own musical inadequacy. I am happy to recognize and respond to the expertise of others in this field. However, it is clear that for a variety of reasons relationships between clergy and organists are not always right. Furthermore, it is clear that there is a great turmoil in the Church over music generally.

I very much welcome *Weary And Ill At Ease*, based as it is upon long experience and careful research. The Anglican musical tradition is one of the glories of the world. Although it flowers and blossoms in cathedrals, it is rooted in the parish church, however small. It is, therefore, important that this outstanding tradition of music should be kept alive and the appropriate excellence fostered.

It is no less obvious that we need new music today. Much is being produced, but alas a good deal of this is banal, ephemeral in the extreme, or totally unmemorable. Yet every now and again new words and new music combine to produce something really worthwhile, which becomes accepted right across the churches. Good new music and good new writing need to be encouraged. In short, we need as always the best of the old and the best of the new. Every generation is different and our perception of what is the best will not necessarily be the same as that of our forebears. So there is a constant shifting of taste. Yet some things endure and others are rediscovered.

In the changing, sometimes difficult, but potentially creative situation that we are now in as far as music in Church is concerned, it is very good to have *Weary And Ill At Ease*. I wish it well. May it help all those involved in the musical life of the Church to raise our hearts to God in joy.

+ Richard Oxon

Preface

The preamble to the BBC radio quiz *I'm Sorry, I Haven't A Clue* describes the programme as an antidote to panel games. The official Report of the Archbishops' Commission on Church Music, *In Tune With Heaven*, was published only a few months ago, and some may consider *Weary And Ill At Ease* to be an antidote to official reports. This is not to say that there is anything wrong with official reports, as indeed there is nothing wrong with panel games. I hope that the two books, written from their different viewpoints and in their different styles, will be seen as complementing one another.

How did this book come about? For over 30 years I have been a regular churchgoer, usually, but not always, singing in the choir. On many occasions and in widely differing circumstances I have seen music cease to be a force for unity, and become instead an occasion for division — with disastrous consequences for all concerned.

Many of my evangelical friends would argue that the root cause of such division is sin. In a sense, no doubt, they are right. However, as well as being a Christian by persuasion, I am a scientist by training, and for some time I have wondered whether a systematic study might not throw some much needed light on the matter. It seemed unlikely that anyone else would ever embark on such a study and, when it became clear that my employer, the University of Oxford, would allow me to work part-time, and that through a family legacy I could afford to do so, I grasped the opportunity with both hands. This book is based upon the work that I undertook for a PhD degree, awarded in 1991 by the University of Sheffield.

I have been fortunate in certain freedoms normally denied to authors of official reports. The opinions and conclusions here are entirely my own, though they have been reached after discussion with colleagues and friends. I have sometimes strayed beyond my stated brief, either because some piece of information is spread over many different publications, or because it is not published at all. Finally, and I think this important, I have tried where possible to make the book entertaining. As jester Jack Point reminds us:

> When they're offered to the world in merry guise,
> Unpleasant truths are swallowed with a will—
> For he who'd make his fellow-creatures wise
> Should always guild the philosophic pill![1]

Many individuals and institutions assisted in the project, and I am glad to be able to record my thanks to them. Firstly I am most grateful to my research supervisors Dr Alan Brown and Professor Edward Garden. The book *Rural Anglicanism* by the Revd Dr Leslie Francis (now Professor) first suggested to me the feasibility of my project: I thank him for that, and for sharing with me his experience in the design and use of questionnaires. I am indebted also to Canon Vincent Strudwick. He not only allowed the project to take place in the Oxford Diocese, but actively encouraged it, smoothing my path to the door of many a Rural Dean.

I am grateful too for help from many others, including Bryan Anderson, Dr Penny Atkinson, Lin Barnetson, Ronald Bayfield, Harry Bramma, Clive Bright, Gerald Burton, Mervyn Byers, Dr Lionel Dakers, Canon Arthur Dobb, Roger Doughty, Canon Anthony Gann, Geoffrey Gleed, Dr Mark Gretason, Dr Paul Griffiths, Dr Berkeley Hill, Geoff-

---

[1] W.S. Gilbert: *The Yeomen Of The Guard.*

rey Holroyde, Dr Roger Homan, Tony Hunter, Michael Keeling, the Revd David Manship, the Revd Geoff Maugham, the Very Revd Michael Mayne, Richard Osmond, Geoff Palmer, David Peacock, Doreen Peters, Betty Rees, Dr Dave Rossiter, Anthony Russell, Patrick Russill, the Revd Christopher Rutledge, Katy Semper, Robin Sheldon, Dr Chris Spencer, Sheridan Swinson, Bill Tamblyn, the late Canon Cyril Taylor, Ian Traynar, Andrew Underwood, Canon William Vanstone, Vincent Waterhouse, Roger Wilkes, Dr John Winter and Dr Jim Wrightson.

I also wish to thank those institutions which contributed grants towards the expenses of the project: Bedford College [London] Association Special Fund Trust, Culham Educational Foundation, the Diocese of Oxford, the Music in Worship Trust, the Royal School of Church Music, and J. Wippell and Company Ltd.

No questionnaire, however well planned, can be of any use without the co-operation of the respondents. I was most fortunate in this, and wish to record my thanks to all those who took the time and trouble to complete them. One hard-pressed clergyman actually completed eight.

Most of all, my thanks go to Ceridwen for her forbearance. When I began the project, two months after our getting married, neither of us realised just how much time I would be spending on it. I was also blessed with two faithful companions during the many 'slow watches of the night' that I spent at the word processor — our dogs Judy and Sheba. My most recent 'assistant' by day has been our baby daughter Bethan, who on several occasions joined me on my lap as I typed.

Introduction

Few issues arouse such strong feelings as those relating to religious belief. Newspapers are not sparing in their reports of the discussion of such issues — especially if that discussion seems in any way acrimonious.

Issues confronting the Church of England in recent years have included: Anglo-Catholic versus Evangelical (perhaps leading ultimately to unity with either Rome or the Free Churches); charismatic versus non-charismatic (dictating the degree of adherence to liturgy); liberal versus conservative (dictating how literally scripture should be interpreted); arguments for and against disestablishment (does an 'official' Church, with its bishops in the House of Lords, speak with greater or less authority — especially if the final selection of those bishops rests with a possibly atheist prime minister?); the rights and wrongs of the Church (especially the Established Church) 'meddling' in national politics; and finally, perhaps in the short term most divisive: the movements for and against the ordination of women as priests.

In addition to these many controversies there has been the age-old debate on the role of music in worship. My principal aim in this book is to examine the current state of that debate. In particular I have tried, by means of a large-scale questionnaire survey, to obtain the views from those who are often regarded as the 'party leaders', namely clergy on the one hand, and church organists and musical directors on the other.

In this Introduction we look at the fundamental issues of the debate before placing them in the context of the present day. We also cast a sidelong glance at other related areas of concern. Mine is far from being the only survey of church music undertaken since World War II, and the Introduction concludes with a review of the other surveys, notably that of the recent Archbishops' Commission on Church Music.

Much has happened to affect music in the Church of England in the last 30 years, notably liturgical changes, culminating in *The Alternative Service Book 1980*, and an 'explosion' of hymns and other congregational music. In Chapter 1 we examine not only these, but also the means of coming to terms with them, namely courses and qualifications in church music. Moving from the general to the particular, in Chapter 2 I sketch three case studies in which either the vicar or the organist (or both) failed to come to terms with the situation. The remainder of the chapter describes how the questionnaire survey was managed. Chapters 3–7 contain the results of the survey, namely the personal backgrounds and general attitudes of clergy and organists, and their perceptions, both objective and subjective, of the situation at their church, and of each other. Also in Chapter 7 I attempt to draw certain conclusions for improving clergy-organist relationships.

Points of Departure

Temperley describes how, throughout the history of Christianity, there have been conflicting currents between those holding different views on the use of music in worship.

> There have always been those who recognise the great emotional power of music to move men's spirits. Some have as a consequence come to mistrust this mysterious power and to exclude it altogether from worship, in spite of clear biblical injunctions to praise God with psalms, and hymns, and spiritual songs, and with instruments of music (e.g. Psalm 150:3–5; Colossians 3:16). This

was the attitude of the Quakers and, for a time, of the General Baptists, but it has never found appreciable support in the Church of England, except perhaps from the unmusical.

Others, also acknowledging the emotional power of music, have been concerned to harness it for the good of men's souls. This view has been held by Lutherans, Puritans, Evangelicals, and Tractarians; it has led to a concern that music should be sung earnestly and spontaneously by the entire congregation, and that both the text sung and the music itself should be appropriate to the purpose — but of course, opinions have varied widely as to what music is appropriate.

A third body of opinion denies the role of music as an actual vehicle of religious expression, but values it as an ornament in the offering to God, as a part of the 'beauty of holiness'. . . . In the English parish church, the conflict between the second and third of these views remains unresolved. There has never been full agreement as to whether the primary goal is for people to sing the music as well as they can, or for the music to be the best possible. It will be found that this issue lies at the back of most of the conflicts and difficulties that have punctuated the history of parish church music.[1]

Long considers the difficulties of reconciling the second and third views:

In order to be sung by all conditions of men, melodies must move mainly by step . . . must be restricted in range, elementary in rhythm and easy to memorise. Admittedly there are many splendid tunes that do satisfy these requirements but in the long run such restrictions must eventually become a strait jacket, stifling vitality and imagination and tending towards uniformity and monotony.[2]

Long's definition of the third group appears to be more tolerant than that adopted by Temperley:

Song is a natural outlet for the expression of our noblest and deepest feelings and when these feelings are of worship, praise and thanksgiving to Almighty God, we are woefully conscious of

---

[1] Nicholas Temperley, *The Music of the English Parish Church* (CUP, Cambridge, 1979), p. 4.

[2] Kenneth R. Long, *The Music of the English Church* (Hodder and Stoughton, London, 1972), pp. 34–35.

how inadequate even our utmost skill is to convey all that is in
our hearts without having that expression arbitrarily scaled down
to what less gifted people can do. Such artificial limitations and
restrictions must inevitably give way as we open the flood-gates
of pent-up emotions.

Long goes on to describe what might be termed a cycle in
religious music, a phenomenon common to other art forms:

> Musical people tend, often unconsciously, to . . . elaborate simple
> basic material to a point where less musical folk can no longer
> participate. . . . The development of church music has often been
> a sinuous line between the musicians, who were constantly
> enriching it with new conceptions, advancing techniques and
> increasing resources (sometimes to the point of extravagance); and
> the reformers, like Pope John XXII, Cranmer, Calvin, the Council
> of Trent, and others, who tried to constrain it and prevent excess.

In short, music may be seen not just as an *aid* to worship,
but actually as a *form* of worship, expressing realities that
mere words are quite incapable of conveying. As our old
friend the Revd. Septimus Harding, Precentor of Barchester,
put it:

> If there is no music, there is no mystery. If there is no mystery,
> there is no God. If there is no mystery, there is no faith.[1]

It seems very unlikely, however, that those in Temperley's
first two groups would agree with him on this point.

The Church's Response

One of the marvels of the Anglican Church has been the
parallel development of two independent, but complementary, streams of church music. The *parish-church tradition*,
which in general encourages active congregational participation in most if not all of the singing, is close to the ideal of

[1] Alan Plater, *The Barchester Chronicles*, a television dramatisation based on
The Warden and *Barchester Towers* by Anthony Trollope (BBC, London,
1979).

Temperley's second group. The third group will often take delight in the *cathedral tradition* (and that of collegiate and royal chapels), where the music is greater both in extent and complexity, and is sung by a choir whose adults nowadays are frequently the holders of musical degrees or diplomas. At such services, the aim is that worship is offered by the choir on behalf of the congregation, since it would clearly be impracticable for members of the congregation to join in the singing, other than the hymn(s). Indeed at certain cathedrals even this seems to be discouraged!

Although the division into parish-church and cathedral traditions is in general helpful, it should certainly not be seen as absolute. Long describes the situation at cathedrals in the first half of the nineteenth century:

> Since senior clergy had no interest whatsoever in cathedral worship and its music, they saw little point in wasting money on it. As a consequence choirs were so reduced in size that it became impossible for them to fulfil their proper function. St. Paul's, which at one time had had 42 choirmen, was now reduced to six.[1]

In 1841, when music in cathedrals was at its nadir, Leeds Parish Church instituted fully choral services in the cathedral tradition, sung by a robed professional choir of men and boys. Many parish churches, to a greater or lesser extent, in due course followed the example of Leeds. Indeed, the revival of choral music in the Anglican Church during the second half of the century came initially not from the cathedrals but from the parish churches.[2]

The period 1900–70 was marked by a great improvement in the musical standards of all church choirs. Long attributes this to the work of the training and examining bodies, and the opportunities afforded by radio and gramophone to hear church music well performed. On the other hand, since the

---

[1] Long, p. 320.
[2] Long, p. 331.

end of World War II, parish choirs had been experiencing
ever-increasing difficulties in recruitment.[1]

Seeds of Conflict

In recent years, many have written of a breakdown in
relations between clergy and organists. While still organist
at Exeter Cathedral, Lionel Dakers was already expressing
his concern:

> There is something in the make-up of clergy and organists which
> on occasion impels them to behave both irresponsibly and
> irrationally. Obvious to all are the repercussions of two apparently
> responsible adults, both in prominent parochial positions, being
> unable to see eye to eye. Much harm can be done to the cause of
> the Church by the inevitable tongue wagging which accompanies
> such incidents.[2]

It was a topic to which, as Director of the Royal School of
Church Music, he was to return on several occasions:

> To tolerate and respect the other point of view and to be prepared
> to act on it, is difficult for many clergy and organists. The fact
> that music is ultimately the legal responsibility of the parson has
> been known to result in a misplaced power complex, especially if
> the incumbent is unsure of his ground.[3]

> A good working relationship is the more essential today if only
> because issues virtually unknown a generation ago now loom
> large. Changes in the shape and language of services inevitably
> rub off on the music and the musicians, and friction can arise the
> more easily. Nowadays, both sides so readily feel threatened and
> consequently tend to react from a position of insecurity. In

---

[1] Long, p. 388.

[2] Lionel Dakers, *Church Music at the Crossroads* (Marshall, Morgan and Scott, London, 1970), p. 86.

[3] Lionel Dakers, *A Handbook of Parish Music* (Mowbray, London, 1976), p. 45.

practice it matters not whether this threat is in fact real or imaginary.[1]

On the closely related subject of relations between the clergy and the choir, he wrote:

Whatever conclusions may have been arrived at concerning the validity of a choir and whether it may have genuinely become outmoded in the face of an agreed change of policy in a church, a situation sometimes fuelled by the choir being adamant in refusing to concede one iota, those responsible for the dismantling process often seem to act in a particularly unsympathetic and frequently pre-emptory way. . . .

What in the event frequently conspires is that the clergy, sometimes encouraged by elements within the congregation, adopt bulldozing tactics resulting in summary dismissal, this being the convenient weapon for a quick kill which causes the greater hurt to the recipients. Little account is taken, or probably contemplated, of the effect of suddenly cutting musicians off from fulfilling the particular gifts they wish to offer towards the enrichment of worship. This is the more wounding when gifted musicians are alienated and, as a result, sometimes permanently lost to the Church.[2]

Were the problems really as great as Dakers would lead us to believe? After only six months in the post, his successor was already writing:

Before I came to work at the RSCM I had often heard of break-down in relationships between clergy and organists, but had never experienced one at first hand. I had been fortunate in every one of the eight places of worship where I had been organist to have enjoyed a friendly working partnership with the priest in charge. Could all these stories be true, I often asked myself? Alas — I now know they are. Hardly a week passes at Addington without a letter or telephone call relating to yet another incident of a kind which is becoming increasingly common. Disagreements there have always been. But it seems the kind of tensions experienced today

---

[1] Lionel Dakers, *Church Music in a Changing World* (Mowbray, Oxford, 1984), p. 76.

[2] Lionel Dakers, 'Aspects of a questioning age' in *Church Music Quarterly*, July 1987, p. 3.

are more than differences of opinion. So often there seems to be a complete breakdown of understanding in which ignorance, fear, insensitivity and unwillingness to change all feature.[1]

Others have expressed similar concern, although not always from the same viewpoint. Here is the view of a clergyman from the charismatic wing of the Church:

> If you were to do a survey among Anglican vicars as to who was public enemy number one in their church, how many would say the organist or the choirmaster? I suspect a very high proportion. I'm not sure whether the same is true in non-conformist circles, but in the Church of England there is often a fierce rivalry between the musical side of the church and its vicar; a rivalry which has been responsible for more than a few nervous breakdowns on both sides.[2]

Meanwhile, in a leaflet edited by a group of clergy in the Oxford Diocese there appeared the comment: 'The parson may have his freehold, but the organist may have a stranglehold on the parish.'[3]

Any thoughts that this problem may be confined to the Church of England are quickly dispelled in a paper by Moores:

> At a recent meeting of the American Guild of Organists in St Petersburg, Fla., a regional officer began her speech on clergy-organist relationships with an observation about how widespread problems are in this area, singling out the Episcopal Church as the church where the clergy-organist relationship is characteristically the most tense.[4]

He goes on to suggest that musicians and clergy possess surprisingly similar types of personality:

[1] Harry Bramma, 'Clergy and organists... fellow workers' in *Church Music Quarterly*, October 1989, p. 10.

[2] John Leach, *Liturgy and Liberty* (MARC, Eastbourne, 1989), p. 81.

[3] 'The Lost Accord' in *Parish and People*, 27 (1986), [p. 2]. We will be examining this further on page 125.

[4] The Revd Dr David R. Moores, 'Clergy-Organist Relationships' in *The American Organist*, August 1985, pp. 46–47.

As highly intuitive types, both clergy and musicians deal with the world and make decisions more often using information best described as subjective, not hard facts or objective data. This use of the subjective opens both types to much greater creativity and imagination, but it also causes them to act much more decisively on the basis of their feelings alone.

The important role that intuition plays is complicated by the fact that both church musicians and clergy preside over 'mysteries'. Who understands the evocative power of music? Who understands the evocative power of ritual? Yet clergy and musicians preside over these complementary mysteries (and ministries), and while there is great mutual respect, there can be an underlying element of insecurity and fear, which causes each minister subconsciously or consciously to wish to control the other.

Moores believes that many clergy view their relationships with organists as a marriage in which the latter must 'love, honour and *obey*'. A much more healthy view of the relationship is as a partnership in which the clergy are senior partners:

As caring partners, there must be constant, effective communication . . . which must be concrete and specific. This requires honesty and candour. Each needs to know (not just sense) what the other thinks and feels. For until each knows (not just senses) where the other stands on all the substantive issues pertaining to music and liturgy, there will be no significant development of a long-range relationship.

He then proposes a radical way of improving the relationship:

Whether or not the clergy compliment you the musician, you can compliment them. . . . It is true that clergy often develop better defences so as to appear self-sufficient, strong and authoritative, but they thrive on praise as much as anyone. . . .

Those who have worked with clergy who are suffering from 'burnout' know that one of the chief causes of such personal anguish is lack of nurturing. Clergy find themselves (or put themselves) in roles which make them the primary nurturer in the parish, and very few lay people, let alone musicians, do anything substantive to help them. Here the musician is in a unique position to do some ministry for the minister and, in so doing, *both* can be blessed.

The spiritual blessing which can come from affirmation is obvious, and so is a very practical blessing. The behaviour of the clergy towards a personally affirming musician will doubtlessly be less arbitrary and authoritarian. To put it bluntly, you do not fire a member of your team who regularly strives to make you feel good.

In conclusion, Moores points out that much of what he has written applies to any relationship, but that in this particular instance the stakes are very high:

It is not too dramatic to say that we deal with eternal verities; our concern is the health and vitality of the soul of man.

Other Matters of Concern

The shortage of organists was already being described as 'grave' more than thirty years ago.[1] In an attempt to combat it, the Royal School of Church Music, the Royal College of Organists, and five other institutions combined to designate 1990 as 'National Learn-the-Organ Year'. The aims were: to encourage at least 500 musicians to take up the organ; to link pupils with competent teachers of the organ in their home areas; and to initiate the publication of a new British organ tutor. The event proved to be an outstanding success.[2] The continuing advancement of electronic-keyboard instruments may well encourage others in the direction of the organ console.

Electronic organs have been at the centre of further controversy recently:

It has, until now, been editorial policy to refuse advertisement of electronic organs in *Church Music Quarterly*. . . . As part of its

---

[1] *Music in Church*, Report of the Committee appointed in 1948 by the Archbishops of Canterbury and York (Church Information Board, Westminster, 1951); revised edition (CIB, Westminster, 1957), p. 79.

[2] Anne Marsden Thomas, 'National Learn-the-Organ Year 1990' in *Church Music Quarterly*, April 1991, pp. 12–13.

efforts to increase the relevance of *CMQ* to the interests of church musicians, the Council thinks that the time is right to reverse a policy which in 1990 at best seems paternalistic, at worst an unusual form of censorship.[1]

This led to a stern rebuke from one of the traditionalists:

Pseudo simulators may indeed be improving all the time, but no improvement to a plastic flower ever made it a rose. And so, we are instructed, no improvement to a lie ever made it true, although much research is currently going into this. Those that have ears to hear, let them hear; otherwise *caveat emptor*.[2]

Bramma has cited as 'a frequent cause of severe disagreement in our churches'[3] the introduction of girls into a previously all-male choir. On the one hand, it is unfair to exclude them from exercising a musical ministry. On the other, at least in urban churches, Bramma observes that introducing girls to the choir invariably causes a number of the boys (the counter-tenors, tenors and basses of tomorrow) to leave. He sees no alternative but to run two complementary choirs which sing together at major festivals.

In 1984 it was decided that St. Edmundsbury, the only English cathedral to admit girls to the choir, would no longer do so. The organist, Harrison Oxley, resigned in protest.[4] Now, however, further consideration is being given to the use of girls in cathedral choirs:

Richard Shephard, headmaster of the Minster School in York and a member of the Archbishops' Commission on Church Music, told the annual conference [of the Choir Schools Association] that no one knew the sort of noise girls could make, because no girls had ever been trained in the same way as boys. He quoted evidence to

---

[1] Sir John Margetson, 'Electronic organs' in *Church Music Quarterly*, October 1990, p. 3.

[2] Bruce Buchanan (Director of J.W. Walker & Sons, Organ Makers), an open letter to the Director of the RSCM, published as an advertisement in *Church Music Quarterly*, October 1990, p. 2.

[3] Harry Bramma, 'Clergy and organists... fellow workers' in *Church Music Quarterly*, October 1989, p. 11.

[4] 'Cathedral choir to drop girls' in *Church Times*, 6330 (8 June 1984), p. 8.

the Commission from the Royal Academy of Music which claimed
that prejudice against girls' voices was founded on musical ignorance.[1]

Meanwhile Richard Seal, with the approval of the Dean and
Chapter, proceeded to launch a fund for the introduction for
a girls' choir at Salisbury Cathedral.[2] This began singing in
the autumn of 1991. Information on a survey of the use of
girls' voices in cathedral choirs has recently been published[3], and an experiment of allowing women to sing in
them has also been proposed.[4] I know at least three suitable
candidates who would be delighted to help remedy any
shortage of male altos! The analogy with women deacons,
now increasingly ministering in cathedrals, should not be
overlooked.

In recent years two other controversial departures have
been reported: Barry Rose from St. Paul's in 1984,[5] and
Simon Preston from Westminster Abbey in 1987.[6] In both
cases it was reported that differences with the Dean and
Chapter over musical policy were to blame. A chilling
comment appeared in *Church Music Quarterly*:

> If those directly concerned with cathedral music are wise. . . they
> will not grow complacent. . . . There are many clergymen, some
> of them in quite senior positions, who care very little for maintain-
> ing that 'unique national choral tradition', insofar as it provides a
> good reason for cathedrals and other foundations to allocate large
> sums of cash to maintain superb choirs. Some of these clergymen,
> moreover, even reject the notion that a fine choir enhances the
> beauty and holiness of cathedral worship in a significantly more
> impressive way than, say, an amateur folk group would do. The

[1] Betty Saunders, 'Girl choristers need same training as boys, choir schools
urged' in *Church Times*, 6641 (25 May 1990), p. 3.
[2] 'Sweet singing in the choir' in *Church Times*, 6641 (25 May 1990), p. 7.
[3] Judith Pearson, 'Equal opportunities?' in *Church Music Quarterly*, July 1992,
pp. 18–19.
[4] Jennifer Zarek, 'The Bavin Report' in *Church Times*, 6744 (15 May 1992),
p. 11.
[5] 'Master of St. Paul's choir quits' in *Church Times*, 6334 (6 July 1984), p. 1.
[6] 'Move from Abbey' in *Church of England Newspaper*, 4850 (15 May 1987),
p. 16.

five centuries of inspiring repertoire, upon which a cathedral choir
can draw, is used as an argument against, not for, their continuation: a sign that they are inextricably linked with the ancient
ways of worship which most parishes jettisoned with the 1662
Prayer Book.

So far, this has manifested itself in a few, comparatively minor,
local disputes: mysterious resignations by cathedral organists;
rumours of anti-musical pressures from domineering Deans. In 20
years' time, however, when the present generation of parish priests
has moved into positions of authority, wholesale changes in
cathedrals could be underway.[1]

Canterbury Cathedral found itself in the middle of a
controversy concerning the enthronement of Dr George
Carey as Archbishop of Canterbury in April 1991. The
controversy surrounded the Archbishop's choice of music,
and led to such headlines in the national tabloids as: 'Pray,
make the go-go gospel go with a swing'. The more sedate
members of the Church of England were no doubt aghast to
read over their breakfast:

Hand-clapping evangelical 'Gospel songs' will be sung to an
accompaniment of guitars and a saxophone. . . in an unprece-
dented break with tradition. . . . The decision has astonished
musical traditionalists, who argue that it could destroy the solemn
atmosphere inside the cathedral.[2]

But reassurance was close at hand.

Evangelical songs and charismatic hand-claps will not prevent 'the
unique English choral tradition' from shining through at the
Archbishop of Canterbury's enthronement next Friday. Guitars,
saxophone and the sound of an electronic keyboard will not drown
the trumpet fanfare of the Royal Marines. The Dean of

---

[1] Richard Morrison, 'A pinnacle, not an ivory tower' in *Church Music Quarterly*, July 1989, p. 3.
[2] Damian Thompson, 'Saxophone and guitars will enthrone Carey' in *The Daily Telegraph*, 42234 (8 April 1991), p. 2.

Canterbury, the Very Revd John Simpson, gave the assurance this week in answer to criticisms of music chosen by Dr Carey.[1]

The Cathedral choir would be singing Parry's *I was glad* and a new setting of the *Te Deum* by Grayston Ives, while the congregational hymns would be to 'well-known melodies from the centre of English tradition'. Even the break with tradition would not be too drastic:

> 'Also taking part, at Dr Carey's personal request, is the All Souls' Ensemble under the direction of Noel Tredinnick, which will sing three songs at that informal moment in the service when the congregation exchange the Peace and the Archbishop greets the ecumenical guests.'

Other Surveys of Church Music

Three times this century the Archbishops of Canterbury and York have asked a group to investigate church music. The Reports of the ensuing *Committees* appeared in 1922[2] and 1951: that of the *Commission* (also known as ACCMUS) in May 1992. The foreword to the 1951 Report began:

> In 1922 the Archbishops of Canterbury and York appointed a strong Committee 'to consider and report upon the place of music in the worship of the Church, and in particular the training of church musicians, and the education of the clergy in the knowledge of music as a branch of liturgical study'.[3]

Seventy years on from the first Report we read:

> [We recommend that] dioceses and parishes consider the provision of local in-service training courses for church musicians. . . [and

---

[1] 'Choral tradition safe at Canterbury service' in *Church Times*, 6687 (12 April 1991), p. 2.

[2] *Music in Worship*, Report of the Archbishops' Committee appointed in May 1922, (Central Board of Finance and SPCK, London, 1923), revised edition (Press and Publications Board of the Church Assembly, London, 1932).

[3] *Music in Church*, Report of the Committee appointed in 1948 by the Archbishops of Canterbury and York (Church Information Board, Westminster, 1951); revised edition (CIB, Westminster, 1957).

that] theological colleges and courses, as well as those responsible
for post-ordination training and continuing ministerial training,
review their provision for the training of ordinands and clergy in
the art of preparing for and conducting public worship, and the use
of worship within it.[1]

Much of my own research underlines this need, but I
question whether ACCMUS will be any more effective in
achieving this objective than its two predecessors.

The announcement in July 1988 of the creation of the
Commission gave rise to much comment — in the national as
well as the church press — with such headlines as 'Church
faces up to pop music challenge' and even 'Sounding an
Almighty sour note in the aisles'. In order to stimulate
debate on the subject, *Church Music Quarterly* invited a
number of musicians to suggest points which the Commission ought to be considering.[2] They included Peter Aston,
who was concerned at current standards of church music,
especially in evangelical churches:

> Why is it so feeble? A case in point is at our own university
> chaplaincy in Norwich. I have been frankly appalled that even my
> music students, who apply normal critical standards and strive for
> the highest possible quality of performance when giving concerts,
> are content to play inferior music badly in their campus services.
> When I question them I am told that 'sincerity is all that matters'.

Simon Preston's concern was twofold.

> I don't think that the Church has ever addressed itself to pro-
> fessional musicians; it has never decided what its attitude to them
> is. Perhaps this is part of a bigger problem, that the clergy cannot
> come to terms with the laity in general, or harness the very real
> skills that the laity possesses. . . . I do hope that this Commission
> will *investigate*, and not simply accept and endorse the changes of

---

[1] *In Tune With Heaven*, Report of the Archbishops' Commission on Church
Music (Church House Publishing, and Hodder and Stoughton, London, 1992),
pp. 257–8.

[2] Peter Aston et al, 'What should they be talking about?' in *Church Music
Quarterly*, October 1988, pp. 4–7.

the last few years — the *ASB* in particular, of course — which have
so affected the work of musicians.

John Barnard, one of the music editors of *Hymns for
Today's Church*, feared that the Commission might attempt
too much.

> On the one hand, I hope that the Commission will feel free to say
> straightforwardly and fearlessly what they think about the current
> state of Anglican music, and to give clear recommendations for
> the future. On the other, I hope they will not lose sight of the fact
> that their deliberations will be pointless unless they lead to a
> response in the churches. That can only come about if they gain
> the respect and confidence of church musicians in general.

In addition to making 56 recommendations for the future of
church music (of which the training of clergy and church
musicians are but two), the 320-page ACCMUS Report
reviews many aspects of the use of music in worship. These
include parish churches, cathedrals, religious communities,
schools, the Church overseas and Churches of other denominations, musical instruments and equipment, radio, television
etc. and copyright. One of the recommendations is that 'the
Royal School of Church Music be recognised as the Church
of England's official body for church music, on the understanding that it continue to broaden its approach to church
music and that it be related in some way to the General
Synod'[1] — an interesting example of privatisation in reverse.
However, the overall tone of its findings may be gleaned
from the following:

> . . . the outlook for music in the Church of England is an uncer-
> tain and, in many ways, disturbing one. Although there is much
> that is positive and encouraging, a sad picture emerges of a
> dwindling supply of musicians, a reduced use of other than
> congregational music, a considerable lowering of standards, and
> a lack of both resources and expectations. The overall impression
> gained by the Commission is that the Church in general either

---

[1] *In Tune With Heaven*, p. 257.

takes for granted the contribution of music to its worship, or places little value on it.[1]

Reviews of the Report in the national press suggested that the root cause of the problem lies not so much in church music itself, as in the decline in church attendance[2] although, to be fair, the Commission by implication addresses this point:

> Some church musicians, and the clergy and congregations to which they belong, may feel that many of the suggestions made in this Report are not for them. The Commission's description of a director of music may seem laughably idealistic to a parish which can barely find a 'reluctant organist'; some of the resources here described as necessary are likely to be dismissed as wholly unrealistic by a church with a handful of worshippers struggling to meet its diocesan quota, as well as to repair its roof.

The critical question is just how many churches come into this category. My own research suggests that it is a substantial number — we shall be looking at this on page 115. At first reading, Bishop Colin Buchanan 'learned virtually nothing about what is [currently being] sung', and could find 'no solid discussion' on music groups[3]. Perhaps there will be a sequel in *Church Music Quarterly* in which contributors to the earlier article can give their views on the Report. Returning to the fears expressed by John Barnard, I hope that the Report's title: *In Tune With Heaven* will not alienate those whose church-music preferences do not lie with Parry or Milton.[4] The Report also carries a summary of the results of a questionnaire survey organised on behalf of ACCMUS.

---

[1] *In Tune With Heaven*, p. 171.

[2] Ruth Gledhill, 'Churches dance to a new tune' in *The Times*, 64328 (9 May 1992), p. 5; also Tom Sutcliffe, 'From whence the divine inspiration?' in *The Guardian* (14 May 1992), p. 22.

[3] Colin Buchanan, Editorial in *News of Liturgy* (Grove, Nottingham, 1992), p. 1.

[4] The front cover shows a page of the score of C.H.H. Parry's *Blest Pair of Sirens*, a setting of *At a Solemn Music* by John Milton. The page contains the words: 'and keep in tune with Heaven'.

The full results are published separately[1], and we will be examining some of them in subsequent chapters.

Several other surveys on church music have appeared in recent years. In 1976 Temperley organised a short questionnaire in the rural deaneries of Seaford and Selsey in Sussex.[2] This covered such topics as composition and size of the choir, types of music sung by the choir and congregation (including details of hymnals and the degree of usage of 'pop' music), and the instruments and liturgy in use. The deaneries were chosen to permit comparison with the results of questionnaires held in 1853 and 1864 (Seaford), and 1922 (Selsey).

A twelve-page questionnaire was sent with the April 1982 copy of *Church Music Quarterly* to over 5000 correspondents of churches affiliated to the RSCM. It contained a wide range of questions on the church, its choir, the organ, the music sung and the numbers of services, music finance, the choir trainer and organist, and the perceived role of the RSCM. In his report of the project, Hill wrote:

> The results must definitely *not* be interpreted as representing the general state of music in the Church of England; almost certainly the choirs taking part in this survey were among the most active in the denomination as a whole. While it would be wrong to dismiss the music which may (or may not) be happening in unaffiliated Anglican churches as negligible, membership of the RSCM represents such an advantage to active church choirs, not least in pecuniary terms, that *not* to affiliate would be imprudent. The caveat on the nature of the sample must always be borne in mind. Nevertheless the information gathered and presented here is, undoubtedly, the best available on Anglican parish music simply because it is the only available on a wide scale.[3]

---

[1] Jacqui Cooper, *Music in Parish Worship* (Central Board of Finance of the Church of England, London, [dated] 1990 [but not published until 1992]).

[2] Nicholas Temperley, *The Music of the English Parish Church* (Cambridge University Press, Cambridge, 1979), pp. 353–358.

[3] Berkeley Hill, *A Survey of Church Music*, 1982 (Royal School of Church Music, Addington, 1983), p. 2.

At about this time, Winter was conducting a survey of choral liturgical music in the Church of England, with special reference to central London. This included a short questionnaire, sent to clergy, not only in the archdeaconry of London, but also, for purposes of comparison, in the deaneries of Norwich and York. This sought information on liturgies, hymnals, the choir, and the types of musical instruments used.[1]

Administry, the inter-church organisation project, in 1984 held a questionnaire amongst its membership.[2] Unlike Hill's survey, questions invited an essay-type response, covering such areas as hymnals, psalters, song books, choirs, singing groups, information on those holding posts of musical leadership, and the extent to which they determined music policy, and the use of instruments and 'non-congregational' music. The churches taking part appeared to be mainly of an evangelical or charismatic background.

A questionnaire to all members of the Music in Worship Trust was distributed with the Summer 1986 edition of the magazine *Music in Worship*. The results were presented a year later.[3] Apart from seeking members' perceptions of the Trust and its magazine, to a considerable extent the same ground was covered as in the Administry survey. Although there was no question on hymnals, there was one on whether any of the musicians regularly attended music-training courses.

Three surveys of cathedral music have recently been published. One by Hill[4] is similar in character to his earlier survey of music in parish churches. Questionnaires were sent to the organists of all UK Anglican cathedrals (including 'parish church' cathedrals), and those other establishments

[1] John Winter, *Music in London Churches, 1945–1982* (PhD thesis, University of East Anglia, 1984), pp. 228–230.

[2] *A Joyful Noise* (Resource Paper 84:7) (Administry, St. Albans, 1984), pp. 1–20.

[3] 'Results of Your Completed Questionnaire Forms' in *Music in Worship*, 39 (Summer 1987), pp. 4–7.

[4] Berkeley Hill, *The Organisation of Music in Cathedrals in the United Kingdom* (Cathedral Organists' Association, Addington, 1989).

maintaining a cathedral-like choral tradition, such as some
Roman Catholic cathedrals, Oxford and Cambridge college
chapels, and the Royal Peculiars, etc. The second survey is
of the music sung at services at 79 choral foundations in
England, Wales, Scotland and Ireland during 1986. Information on the Responses, Morning and Evening Canticles,
Communion Services and Anthems was compiled from the
cathedral service lists.[1] The survey of female voices in
cathedrals has already been noted on page 12.

Before turning to my own survey, let us first look at the
overall changes in church music over the last 30 years.

---

[1]   John Patton, *Survey of Music and Repertoire* (Friends of Cathedral Music, Chichester, 1990).

1

Through All The Changing
Scenes Of Life[1]

Recent Developments in Church Music

There have been many changes in the Church of England
during the last 30 years — especially when viewed from the
perspective of the organ console. What are these 'changing
scenes', what has caused them, and have they brought
'trouble' or 'joy'? Two separate but related developments
have together affected parish-church music probably more
than at any time since the Reformation.

The first upheaval has been caused by liturgical changes.
After some 300 years of having a fixed liturgy, in the 1960s
the Church of England began to experiment. This culminated
in the publication of *The Alternative Service Book 1980*.[2]
We will begin this chapter by examining how these changes
have affected the music.

In parallel with the liturgical changes, there has been an
'explosion' of hymn writing. We will therefore go on to
review hymns and hymnals.

Dakers emphasises the importance and universality of
hymns:

---

[1] N.Tate and N. Brady, [in, for example,] *Hymns Ancient and Modern Revised*
(Clowes, Beccles, 1950), No. 290.
[2] *The Alternative Service Book 1980* (Clowes, SPCK, CUP, OUP, Mowbray,
and Hodder and Stoughton, London, 1980).

Hymns are everyone's music in church. They are inevitable and they are inescapable. Every so many minutes in almost every act of public worship the entire corpus — clergy, choir and congregation alike — are brought together in a joint preoccupation, that of singing a hymn.[1]

He might easily have added that hymns are very largely interdenominational. Together with the liturgical changes, the hymns generated in the explosion have resulted in a rate of change in church music without parallel since the Reformation. Technology has played its part in this upheaval through the media of radio, television, disc (both conventional and compact), cassette and, indeed, photocopying. In the 'crater' of the explosion, many hymnals have appeared.

The review of hymnals that follows is quite lengthy for three reasons: firstly because of their centrality in worship, secondly because of the absence of a recent wide-ranging review elsewhere, and thirdly (given the title of this book) to demonstrate how the seemingly innocuous publication of a new hymnal can become a subject of controversy, even bitterness. For the sake of completeness, we also look at psalters and speculate on the form that congregational singing books will take in the future.

Finally in this chapter we turn our attention to the training facilities available to help church musicians weather these upheavals.

The Effects of Liturgical Change

Liturgical change evokes a wide variety of responses. There are those who embrace change — any change — with enthusiasm. Worship, they argue, must be expressed in contemporary terms such that the Christian message may be understood by all — those outside the Church as well as those within it — even if the message is sometimes poorly presented aesthetically. Others take a different view. If a form of

---

[1] Lionel Dakers, *Choosing and Using Hymns* (Mowbray, Oxford, 1985), p. 15.

worship has 'stood the test of time', then surely there is little merit in changing it.

Three times in the last 500 years great liturgical upheavals have taken place in Britain: the Reformation, Vatican II, and *The Alternative Service Book 1980*. On each occasion the effects have been far reaching, not least on music and musicians.

We can regard the English Reformation as the period from Henry VIII's break with Rome in 1534, through the publication of Cranmer's first *Book of Common Prayer* in 1549, subsequent editions of 1552 and 1559, to the final edition in 1662. It was a time of great turbulence, as battles to the death were fought between the Papists and Puritans.

The few musicians who did manage to retain or secure appointments in the Henrician Church found themselves faced with almost insuperable difficulties. The Act of Uniformity, which was passed on 21 January 1549, decreed that 'the Book of Common Prayer and none other' was to be used on and after 9 June of that year. This meant that in five months all the plainsong and traditional music built up over the centuries would be ruthlessly swept away, and masses, motets, and all settings of the Latin would become illegal.[1]

It is hard to imagine just how bitter at the time this blow must have been. Yet life had to go on and, in the succeeding years and centuries, composers responded to the command to 'sing a new song to the Lord'[2].

In recent years there has been a 'Reformation' in the Roman Church.

The Roman Catholic Church, for long regarded as the most unchanging of churches, surprised both itself and the world at large by the speed and scale of the changes upon which it embarked in the 1960s. The manner of these changes, however, was characteristic. There was little choice about it; the faithful were told that certain things were going to happen (the most

---

[1] Kenneth R. Long, *The Music of the English Church* (Hodder and Stoughton, London, 1972), p. 26.

[2] *Psalm 96*, v. 1.

spectacular and controversial of which was the introduction of the vernacular), and they did.[1]

In the twenty years following Vatican II, the Roman Rite changed more than it had in the previous fifteen hundred.

> [Before Vatican II] music at 'Sung Mass' (usually one mass per parish per week) would consist of a choral mass setting, generally tuneful but undistinguished, with a motet or two in the same vein and the 'proper' parts sung to a psalm-tone. The full plainchant propers were too difficult for the average choir; such music, and elaborate polyphony, were rare, and congregational singing even rarer. . . . Hymns were not sung; these were reserved for separate Marian and Eucharistic 'devotions'.
>
> Vatican II planted not one but two time bombs in this world. The first was the vernacular, which threatened the entire repertoire of Latin masses and motets, the second was the call to involve the people. The people had not sung at Mass . . . for centuries. . . . In many places the musicians simply found themselves being bypassed by enthusiastic clergy who wanted to get on. Some choirs were disbanded and others were sacked.

The task confronting the Roman Church should not be underestimated.

> It was nothing more or less than the making of a new music for a whole church's liturgy, something not attempted since the Reformation. Music has an enormously important role in the religious 'universe' of the average worshipper, which is why it provokes such strong feelings. To tamper with it is always risky, but to rebuild it is an undertaking which will need much more than the 22 years that have elapsed since the Council.

Seen in the context of the previous two events, the introduction of *The Alternative Service Book 1980* was a very low-key affair. No-one was burnt at the stake, the language of worship had previously been, and still was, the mother tongue, and hymnody remained the most common

---

[1] [Fr] Stephen Dean, 'Roman Catholic Music: the Recent Past and the Future' in *In Spirit and in Truth* (ed. Robin Sheldon) (Hodder and Stoughton, London, 1989), pp. 31–48.

form of musical expression. In any case it was, as its name suggested, only an alternative. That having been said, there must be exceedingly few members of the Church of England who have never encountered the *ASB*. Indeed, for very many congregations it now provides the only form of liturgical worship. How did this come about?

The first real challenge to the *Book of Common Prayer* emerged in the nineteenth century. In 1927 a revised book was agreed by the Church Assembly, but rejected by the House of Commons. After minor changes, a second submission to Parliament suffered the same fate. Undaunted, the bishops took the law into their own hands by publishing the book with a disclaimer that it was not authorised for use in churches, and then issuing a statement effectively inviting clergy to ignore the disclaimer. In this way *The Book of Common Prayer with the additions and deviations proposed in 1928* came into widespread albeit illegal use.

In 1966 the Prayer Book (Alternative and Other Services) Measure was passed by Parliament, enabling the Church to determine its own alternative services, each being for 'optional and experimental use for a period of seven or ten years'. The Church of England (Worship and Doctrine) Measure of 1974 now enables General Synod to regulate all matters relating to worship, provided that the *Book of Common Prayer* remains 'available' and unaltered. However, the precise meaning of 'available' and to whom is unclear: a survey in 1984 demonstrated that in most Anglican theological colleges the *BCP* was seldom or never used.[1]

The 1928 *Prayer Book* was, with minor revision, republished in 1966 under the title *Alternative Services: Series 1*. Meanwhile a Liturgical Commission, appointed in 1955, had produced the first set of its own proposals, and *Alternative Services: Second Series* were approved in 1967/8. The changes introduced in Series 2 were of much greater interest to the theologian or liturgiologist than to the

[1] Dr Roger Homan and Prof. the Revd David Martin, *Theological Colleges and the Book of Common Prayer: a Survey* (Prayer Book Society, London, 1986), pp. 5–10.

church musician or congregation. However, two movements of the mid-1960s: one for ecumenical co-operation, the other for the use of contemporary English in worship, resulted in major overhaul of the liturgy for the Series 3 services, introduced between 1973 and 1979. In turn, these services underwent minor revision, and were published in one volume: *The Alternative Service Book 1980*. The modified Series 3 communion service was given the title of 'Rite A': 'Rite B', a hybrid of Series 1 and 2, was included in the same volume. General Synod approved the use of the *ASB* for an initial period of ten years and, more recently, for a further ten. I wonder whether the *ASB* will be given a further lease of life beyond the year 2000.

Another influence on the *ASB* was the Liturgical Movement, beginning in the Roman Catholic Church on the Continent last century.

> It led to more frequent reception of Holy Communion, [and] a desire for more lay participation in worship. . . . Similar stirrings can be detected in the Church of England in the early years of the twentieth century, but the process really started to get under way . . . with the publication in 1935 of *Liturgy and Society* by A.G. Hebert SSM and two years later a collection of essays, *The Parish Communion*, also edited by Hebert. From this was born 'the Parish Communion Movement', which aimed at restoring the Eucharist as the central act of worship in a parish on a Sunday morning.[1]

However, the Movement's success has not been without a price. In the current shortage of Church of England clergy, it is sometimes necessary for a priest to hurry from church to church on a Sunday morning, in some cases his time of arrival being scheduled to coincide with the prayer of consecration.

The earlier liturgical changes had little impact on the Church's music.[2]   However, as the eighties dawned and

---

[1] R.C.D. Jasper and Paul F. Bradshaw, *A Companion to the Alternative Service Book* (SPCK, London, 1986), pp. 22–23.

[2] The only major change was the inclusion of the 'Benedictus qui venit' and 'Agnus Dei' in the Communion Service of the 1928 *Prayer Book*, after their

'Series 3 Communion' became 'Rite A', with increasing numbers (especially of clergy) committed to it, composers set about the task of writing suitable settings. By 1988 there were at least 44 settings either composed for or suitable for Rite A.[1] The extension of the lifetime of the *ASB* until at least 2000 is likely to encourage further compositions based on this Rite, despite certain inherent difficulties with the text.[2] Although several settings have been written expressly for Rite B, earlier works can be used, more or less without modification.

Owing to the widespread adoption of Parish (or 'Family') Communion, Morning Prayer ('Mattins') is little used. It would appear (page 144) that not merely in Morning Prayer, but in Evening Prayer also, the *BCP* version is more commonly used than that in the *ASB*. Moreover, the custom in parish churches is to sing the canticles to an Anglican chant rather than to a fully choral 'setting'. Such settings tend only to be sung in cathedrals, where the Offices are almost invariably according to the *BCP*. Composers have therefore tended not to write settings for the *ASB* canticles.[3]

General Note 3 of the *ASB* reads: 'Prayer Book Texts. Where parts of a service are sung to well-known settings, the traditional words for which they were composed may be used.' However, such use of traditional texts is rare except in cathedrals, where even Latin settings in an otherwise Rite A service are by no means unknown.

---

exile from the 1552 and 1662 books. However, in practice these items had already been in use for some time in the more catholic churches, and indeed they had both already appeared in, for example, Darke's *Service in F*, published in 1926.

[1] *The Alternative Service Book 1980 (An annotated list of music published by the RSCM and others for: Communion Rite A, Communion Rite B, Canticles, etc.)* (Royal School of Church Music, Addington, 1988), [pp. 3–7, 11–17].

[2] Robert Ashfield, 'The Composer and the *ASB*' in *The Friends of Cathedral Music Annual Report*, 29 (April 1986), p. 28.

[3] One exception is Alan Wilson who, in the *Christus Rex* series, has written settings of all fourteen canticles, in addition to the *Norwich Service* setting of the *Magnificat* and *Nunc Dimittis* (not to mention, at the last count, four Rite A settings).

Although the introduction of the *ASB* did not affect the Church's hymnody, here too changes were afoot, as we will now see.

Hymnals and Psalters

In the last thirty years many new hymnals have appeared. Of these, four major works have been aimed primarily at the Church of England. These are, in chronological order: *Anglican Hymn Book*, *Hymns for Today's Church*, *Hymns Ancient and Modern New Standard Edition*, and *The New English Hymnal*. We will begin by looking at these and, where applicable, their forerunners.

Having passed its silver jubilee, the *Anglican Hymn Book*[1] stands slightly apart from those that were to appear in the 1980s.

> It is many years since a completely new hymn book appeared for use in the Church of England. . . . In making this collection, we have tried to envisage the needs of the whole Church, both now and in the future.

Both the title and the reference in the preface to 'the whole Church' implied a universality lacking in the then current editions of *Hymns Ancient and Modern* and *The English Hymnal*. However, its evangelical outlook could be seen in, for example, the hymn: 'We love the place, O God'. The line 'We love thine altar, Lord' had become 'We love our Father's board'. One innovation, not subsequently adopted by other books, was the inclusion in the metrical index of the first two lines of each tune. The *Anglican Hymn Book* was the first to publish the now famous paraphrase of the Magnificat by Timothy Dudley-Smith: 'Tell out, my soul, the greatness of the Lord'. Leaver writes:

> From today's vantage point the new material presented in *Anglican Hymn Book* may look rather small but to have included about forty new tunes, twenty or so new texts, together with many

[1] *Anglican Hymn Book* (Church Book Room Press, London, 1965).

alternative musical settings was certainly a creditable achievement
for the time, when the modern growth in hymn writing had hardly
begun.[1]

In 1975 a supplement of 49 additional tunes was added, to
be followed in the 1978 reprint by a further 29 hymn texts.
Leaver scornfully refers to these as 'hymnological jerry-
building.' A further supplement, in the form of a separate
volume, *Anglican Praise*[2], contains a hundred hymns, of
which roughly seventy are contemporary. The editors
expressed the hope in the preface that other congregations
besides those using the *Anglican Hymnal* would find the
supplement useful. Cowley[3] has praised the editors for
selecting from a wide range of authors and composers, and
'avoiding the trap fallen into by so many of their illustrious
predecessors — that of including a disproportionate number
of their own hymns and tunes'.

'Great hymns of every age in the language of today': so
ran the pre-publication advertisements for *Hymns for
Today's Church*.[4] In the preface, the consultant editor
Michael Baughen (who had until recently been Rector of All
Souls', Langham Place, London) referred to it as 'the first
major new hymn book of the new era'. This was perhaps
less than fair to the *Anglican Hymn Book*, especially since
in some respects it could be said to be a forerunner of the
newer work. The book contained some 600 hymns. Of these,
about 140 had not previously been published, and more than
100 had appeared in the supplementary hymnals during the
1970s. The remaining hymns were all traditional but, in
most cases, with revised words. Elsewhere in the preface
there was a hint of defensiveness (for example, the changes
in wording of the hymns being referred to as 'invisible
mending'). One of the book's editors went to the extent of

---

[1] Robin Leaver *A Hymn Book Survey 1962–80* (Booklet No. 71) (Grove,
    Nottingham, 1980), p. 8.
[2] Anglican Praise (OUP, Oxford, 1988).
[3] Stephen Cowley, '*Anglican Praise*' in *Christian Music*, Autumn 1988, p. 39.
[4] *Hymns for Today's Church* (Hodder and Stoughton, London, 1982).

writing a separate booklet[1] explaining the reasoning behind
the project.

Much controversy surrounded the official launch of the
work, which took place during General Synod week at a
service in St. Margaret's Westminster — the church of the
House of Commons. Such was the ill-feeling that several
Conservative MPs protested that people 'might think that the
book had the approval of the Commons'.[2] The concern was
twofold. Firstly, the book (like the *Anglican Hymn Book*
before it) was claiming to be for all Anglicans, but in
outlook was very evangelical.[3] In the hymn 'We love the
place, O God', the 'sacred font' had been changed into
'cleansing sign' (the altar already having been banished in
the *Anglican Hymnal* version). The words editor, Michael
Saward, replied that the aim had been to select hymns that
could be sung 'equally by Baptists and Roman Catholics'.[4]

The more controversial issue was the rewriting of the
words. This included changing 'thee' and 'thou' to 'you',
and the removal of archaic endings such as '-est' and '-eth'.
These are illustrated in the hymn 'Immortal, invisible, God
only wise'. The verse:

> To all life thou givest — to both great and small;
> In all life thou livest, the true life of all;
> We blossom and flourish as leaves on the tree,
> And wither and perish — but naught changeth thee.

became:

> To all life you give, Lord, to both great and small,
> in all life you live, Lord, the true life of all:
> we blossom and flourish, uncertain and frail,
> we wither and perish, but you never fail.

---

[1] Christopher Idle, *Hymns in Today's Language* (Booklet No. 81) (Grove,
Nottingham, 1982).

[2] 'New hymnbook compilers give some facts & figures' in *Church Times*, 6248
(12 November 1982) p. 24.

[3] A.B. Robinson, 'Hymns & churchmanship' in *Church Times*, 6252 (10
December 1982), p. 12.

[4] Michael Saward, 'New hymnbook & churchmanship' in *Church Times*, 6253
(17 December 1982), p. 12.

It was perhaps inevitable that a book incorporating changes of this magnitude would lead to controversy. However, the matter which caused a national uproar was the rewriting of the National Anthem in an attempt to remove 'emotive language'. The traditional version of verse one is shown below alongside its revised counterpart:

God save our gracious Queen,	God save our gracious Queen,
Long live our noble Queen,	God bless and guard our Queen,
God save the Queen!	long live the Queen!
Send her victorious,	Guard us in liberty,
Happy and glorious,	bless us with unity,
Long to reign over us;	save us from tyranny:
God save the Queen!	God save the Queen!

At a press conference, Michael Baughen pointed out that the ordinary form of the National Anthem was printed elsewhere in the book.[1]

The polarisation of views concerning the book did not seem to diminish with time. One correspondent referred to 'vandalism . . . done to many well-loved hymns and carols'.[2] In reply, another wrote: 'At last I can sing hymns in the language I speak, which helps me to express what my heart wants to say so much better than the antiquated words of previous centuries.'[3] A third took a cautious view, suggesting that: '[word changing] is good for us, as it focuses our attention on the wording in front of us.'[4] However, this was tempered with the comment, which some might wish to apply also to the *ASB*: 'I suppose change is good but, as in the case of this hymn book, so much concerning the Church of England today appears to be

---

[1] 'New hymnbook compilers give some facts & figures' in *Church Times*, 6248 (12 November 1982) p. 24.

[2] Peter Heath, 'Misled by modern hymns' in *Church of England Newspaper*, 4783 (24 January 1986), p. 10.

[3] Gillian Orpin, 'Grateful for modern hymns' in *Church of England Newspaper*, 4786 (14 February 1986), p. 11.

[4] Hugh Lawson Johnston, 'Word-changing of well-known hymns' in *Church of England Newspaper*, 4785 (7 February 1986), p. 11.

change solely for the sake of change, which might be
justified if only it was filling our churches.'

> The difficulty . . . as every hymnologist knows, is that hymns
> have been [in a state of] being rewritten since they began. . . . The
> Wesleys protested (not always successfully) against having their
> own hymns rewritten; but they were ready enough to rewrite the
> works of lesser hymnodists. And few people would now blame
> them. . . . In the end, it all depends on who's doing the rewrit-
> ing.[1]

The following appeared a few weeks after the hymnal's
publication:

> *Hymns for Today's Church* must be the last hymn book to be
> published in our generation. Our generation needs not bound hymn
> books designed to last for ten years but loose-leaf compilations
> that will be able to cope with the torrent of new worship-songs
> that shows no sign of drying up. In twenty or thirty years we shall
> have a fair idea of what is worth keeping. Until then it will be
> prudent to make provisional judgments and to keep our options
> open.[2]

However, this was not to be, as we shall see shortly. In the
second edition, published in 1988, there is a new 'Traditional words' section. However, other hymns have been re-
written on the grounds of the perceived need for inclusive
(non-sexist) language. This has made the two editions
incompatible, a situation which other publishers have
normally managed to avoid. In 1988, the Revd. Christopher
Idle, one of the editors of *Hymns for Today's Church*, was
asked if he had changed his mind concerning the
modernisation of hymns. He admitted: 'Personally I have
retreated from dogmatic rejection of anything archaic.'[3]

---

[1] John Whale, 'It depends who does it' in *Church Times*, 6622 (12 January
    1990), p. 7.
[2] John King, 'Grasping the nettle of hymn copyright' in *Church Times*, 6250
    (26 November 1982), p. 10.
[3] Christopher Idle, 'Twenty Questions about *Anglican Praise*' in *Church of
    England Newspaper*, 4914 (12 August 1988), p. 6.

Hymns Ancient and Modern New Standard[1] was published in 1983 only a few months after *Hymns for Today's Church*, and contained in contrast no original material at all. How had this come about? The story of the first hundred years of *Hymns Ancient and Modern* has been written by Clarke.[2] Since its birth as a product of the Oxford Movement in 1861, it has undergone many revisions and supplements. One of these, in 1904, was widely criticised, in part because of its alteration of words to improve intelligibility[3] (a similar exercise to that attempted more recently in *Hymns for Today's Church*). For example, in the second line of Mrs Alexander's hymn 'There is a green hill', the word 'without' was replaced by 'outside'. Suffice it to say that in all subsequent revisions, including that of 1983, 'without' has been used. The *Standard Edition* (itself containing two supplements) appeared in 1922. Long commented: 'With careful selection . . . even the most discriminating could find a wide range of superb hymns in this curiously patchwork book.'[4] It is a testimony to this edition (described by Routley as 'nothing less than a national institution'[5]) that new copies were on the display shelves of a bookshop in Oxford in 1992, 70 years after publication.

In 1950 there appeared a new edition, entitled *Hymns Ancient and Modern Revised*[6], in which the supplements were finally merged into the main volume, but in such a way that the most popular hymns were allowed to retain their existing numbers. Some hymns were removed either because they had never found favour, or because the editors

[1] *Hymns Ancient and Modern New Standard* (Hymns Ancient and Modern Ltd., Norwich, 1983).
[2] W.K. Lowther Clarke, *A Hundred Years of Hymns Ancient & Modern* (William Clowes, London, 1960).
[3] Marianne Barton, 'From Ancient to Modern' in *Church Music Quarterly*, April 1990, pp. 16–17.
[4] Kenneth R. Long, *The Music of the English Church* (Hodder and Stoughton, London, 1972), p. 400.
[5] Eric Routley, *The Music of Christian Hymnody* (Independent Press, London, 1957), p. 119.
[6] *Hymns Ancient and Modern Revised* (William Clowes, Beccles, 1950).

sensed or even anticipated changes in congregations' tastes. The preface summed up the aspirations of the book:

> [It is hoped that] in this new book the Church will find the same endearing and enduring qualities as in the old, the same heartfelt yet sober tone, so much in keeping with English-speaking Christianity. . . . The book does not aim at breaking fresh ground or exploiting novel ideas.

Long felt that it fully deserved its great popularity.

100 Hymns for Today[1] was one of the first of many supplements to many hymnals. In the Preface, the editors wrote:

> Today's Christians need today's songs as well as yesterday's. . . . Although this book is a collection of hymns for our own time, it does not go so far in the direction of modernity as to include those written in an idiom likely to be so shortlived that any book containing them will be dated within months of publication. We have tried to steer a middle course, therefore, between restatements of the traditional and ephemeral or 'pop' productions.

Examples of 'today's songs' are: 'Living Lord' (Patrick Appleford), 'Sing we a song of high revolt' (Fred Kaan), 'God of concrete, God of steel' (Richard G. Jones), and 'No use knocking on the window' (Sydney Carter), which contains the verse:

> Jesus Christ has gone to heaven;
> One day he'll be coming back, sir.
> In this house he will be welcome,
> But we hope he won't be black, sir.

By 1978, more than a million copies had been sold, which must surely have been a significant factor in the decision to publish a sequel. Strangely, *100 Hymns for Today* lacked an index of first lines, an omission remedied in the sequel. The preface to *More Hymns for Today*[2] set the tone for the work.

---

[1] *100 Hymns for Today* (Clowes, London, 1969).
[2] *More Hymns for Today* (Hymns Ancient and Modern Ltd., Norwich, 1980).

Since [the publication of *100 Hymns for Today*] there has been an unexpected, fresh and exciting output of English hymns, which that supplement may have done something to bring about. . . . Among these recent hymns there are those that have about them something of the elusive quality which seems to mark them with a more enduring character. At least they deserve to be tested for a longer time and introduced more widely in the service of the Church. . . . Like its predecessor, [this] book seeks to be forward looking without abandoning restraint; to be sensitive to the changing needs and renewed vitality of the Church in a turbulent world, while being rooted in the long, living tradition of the people of God.

Again there is a blend of old and contemporary. For example, the hymn 'Sent forth by God's blessing' (Omer Westerndorf, b. 1916) is set to the tune 'The Ash Grove'. A hauntingly beautiful poem, taken from a work by Canon William Vanstone, is set to Song 13 by Orlando Gibbons. However, the text has been altered and, in particular, parts of the first two verses merged to reduce the total number from seven to six. I find this regrettable, especially since there is no reference to the alteration. Here are the first three verses in their original version.[1]

> Morning glory, starlit sky,
> Leaves in springtime, swallows' flight,
> Autumn gales, tremendous seas,
> Sounds and scents of summer night;
>
> Soaring music, tow'ring words,
> Art's perfection, scholar's truth,
> Joy supreme of human love,
> Memory's treasure, grace of youth;
>
> Open, Lord, are these, Thy gifts,
> Gifts of love to mind and sense;
> Hidden is love's agony,
> Love's endeavour, love's expense.

---

[1] W.H. Vanstone, *Love's Endeavour Love's Expense — The Response of Being to the Love of God* (Darton, Longman and Todd, London, 1977), pp. 119–120.

There is also a paraphrase of the Nunc Dimittis by Timothy Dudley-Smith.

> Faithful vigil ended,
>   watching, waiting cease;
> Master, grant thy servant
>   his discharge in peace.[1]

In contrast, there is the American folk hymn: 'Were you there when they crucified my Lord?'. There is also the hymn by the seventeenth-century poet John Mason:

> Now from the altar of our hearts
>   let incense flames arise;
> assist us, Lord, to offer up
>   our morning sacrifice.

It is fun to speculate on what the editors of *Hymns for Today's Church* would have made of that one.

The publication of *Hymns Ancient and Modern New Standard* was a very low-key affair compared with the excitement over *Hymns for Today's Church* a few months earlier. 'For it is seemly so to do' came instinctively to the mind of the reviewer[2], when first browsing through the new work. In the preface she would have read:

English liturgies of the 1980s provide prayers using both the 'Thou' and the 'You' form in address to God or Christ. It has seemed unnecessary to rewrite classical hymns to conform to the 'You' form. Experience suggests that congregations make the adjustment to 'Thou' without difficulty. The feminist movement has also affected attitudes to some hymns. . . . Unlike many other languages, English has only the one word 'man' to carry three distinct meanings: (a) the human race as a whole, (b) an individual human being, (c) an adult male as opposed to a woman or a boy. Some voices of feminine emancipation have come to object to the

---

[1] I have never been able to come to terms with 'discharge'.
[2] Margaret Daniel, 'Judicious pruning' in *Church Times*, 6278 (10 June 1983), p. 7.

first two meanings, not to the third. But we have not thought it right to alter the words of hymns to meet this objection.

The book was produced by selecting just over half of the material in *Hymns Ancient and Modern Revised* and adding all of *100 Hymns for Today* and *More Hymns for Today* onto the end. Many of the earlier hymns were transposed down for the benefit of congregations (but not perhaps altos and basses). In common with practice elsewhere, minims have been replaced by crotchets. There is a list of suitable hymns for the *ASB* Sunday lectionary. Finally, several well-known tunes have been added (for example 'Down Ampney' by Vaughan Williams). It seems strange that the publishers rushed into print only three years after *More Hymns for Today*, allowing those hymns no time for testing before being granted a measure of permanence. It is also surprising that every single one of *100 Hymns for Today* was considered to have passed muster.

New Standard is available in two forms: Complete, and Abridged (that is, without the material from the supplements). The two books *100 Hymns for Today* and *More Hymns for Today* have now been merged into a single volume: *Hymns for Today*. A further recent addition to the family is *Worship Songs Ancient and Modern*[1], bridging, in the words of the editors: 'the present gap between the classic hymn and the popular chorus'.

The fourth major publication aimed towards the Church of England is *The New English Hymnal*.[2] The two main hymn books of the Church of England, *Hymns Ancient and Modern* and *The English Hymnal*[3], have always been regarded as rivals, although this came about by accident. Percy Dearmer and the other compilers of *The English Hymnal* originally wished merely to produce a supplement to *Hymns Ancient and Modern* for the Anglo-Catholic wing

---

[1] *Worship Songs Ancient and Modern* (Canterbury Press, Norwich, 1992).
[2] *The New English Hymnal* (Canterbury Press, Norwich, 1986).
[3] *The English Hymnal* (OUP and Mowbray, London, 1906).

of the Church.[1] However, following the controversy over the 1904 edition, they came under strong pressure to undertake a completely new book which, even then, was not intended as a rival to *Ancient and Modern*. Not surprisingly, the *Ancient and Modern* proprietors felt unable to grant permission to reproduce certain copyright items, which caused the musical editor, Vaughan Williams, to draw on English folk melodies, thereby endowing the book with one of its greatest strengths.

> He drew extensively on three sources practically untapped by previous compilers: sixteenth- and seventeenth-century French 'church melodies', nineteenth-century Welsh Methodist tunes, and English secular folk-songs (or tunes modelled on them). The editor's own contributions included his beautiful 'Down Ampney' ('Come down, O Love divine') and the sturdy 'Sine Nomine' ('For all the saints'), one of the best hymn-tunes of the century. . . . *The English Hymnal* was a marked advance on most previous collections: furthermore, because of the excellence of both words and music, the more cultured and intellectual type of congregation preferred it to the old unreformed *Ancient and Modern*.[2]

Memories sometimes die hard, and it is possible that the refusal of permission by the proprietors of *Ancient and Modern* in 1905 prevented their successors from being allowed in 1950 to use the tunes 'Down Ampney' and 'Sine Nomine' in *Ancient and Modern Revised*.

The thirties brought no more than minor textual and musical changes to *The English Hymnal*.[3] An unsuccessful experiment was the publication of *The English Hymnal Service Book*.[4] Some three hundred hymns taken from *The English Hymnal* were combined with psalms, canticles and other liturgical material. Canon Cyril Taylor commented:

---

[1] Marianne Barton, 'From Ancient to Modern' in *Church Music Quarterly*, April 1990, pp. 16–17.

[2] Kenneth R. Long, *The Music of the English Church* (Hodder and Stoughton, London, 1972), p. 399.

[3] *The English Hymnal* (New Edition) (OUP and Mowbray, London, 1933).

[4] *The English Hymnal Service Book* (OUP, London, 1962).

'Whether this book fulfilled any particular need I have never been able to discover'.[1]

The preface to *English Praise*[2] stated:

> It was at first intended to produce a complete revision of *The English Hymnal* . . . but in a period of liturgical change which might well result in a radical revision of the calendar, it seemed preferable to be content for the time being with a supplement.

As might be expected, this hymnal contains a considerable amount of material that had already seen the light of day in either *Ancient and Modern Revised* or one of its two supplements. However, in common with *The English Hymnal*, many of the hymns are for specific times in the Church's year, for example 'Bitter was the night' (Sydney Carter, Passiontide) and 'The angel rolled the stone away' (Negro spiritual, Easter). One innovation is the inclusion of a small number of responsorial psalms by Dom Gregory Murray. Again, like *The English Hymnal*, the book makes use of English traditional material. An example of this is the carol 'The truth from above', but the editors seem to have been a little careless in the selection of verses.[3] They took the text, without alteration, from *The Oxford Book of Carols*[4], no doubt trusting the judgment of the earlier book's editors, namely Percy Dearmer, Ralph Vaughan Williams, and Martin Shaw. Yet close inspection of the first three verses suggests that something may be missing:

> This is the truth sent from above,
> The truth of God, the God of love,
> Therefore don't turn me from your door,
> But hearken all both rich and poor.

---

[1] Cyril Taylor, 'And still they come' in *English Church Music* (Royal School of Church Music, Addington, 1976), p. 60.

[2] *English Praise* (OUP, London, 1975).

[3] The worst example of this that I ever personally encountered was the annual omission of verse 3 in 'While shepherds watched' at a certain church's carol service.

[4] *The Oxford Book of Carols* (OUP, Oxford, 1928).

The first thing which I do relate
Is that God did man create;
The next thing which to you I'll tell —
Woman was made with man to dwell.

And we were heirs to endless woes,
Till God the Lord did interpose;
And so a promise soon did run
That he would redeem us by his Son.

A still earlier version of the text[1] provides the answer:

. . . . with man to dwell.

Then after this 'twas God's own choice,
To place them both in paradise,
There to remain from evil free.
Except they ate of such a tree.

And they did eat, which was a sin,
And thus their ruin did begin;
Ruined themselves, both you and me,
And all of their posterity.

Thus we were heirs . . .

Whether these verses were omitted accidentally or deliberately from the earlier book is unknown. The former seems unlikely (especially given the change from 'Thus' to 'And'), but the latter seems equally strange, not only because of the logical discontinuity. The carol is clearly intended to tell the story of Creation, the Fall, and Redemption of mankind. To deprive the reader or listener of any one of these is to rewrite Christian theology. The editors of *English Praise* (or *The Oxford Book of Carols*, for that matter) seem scarcely the sort of people who would wish to do so.

Like *Hymns for Today's Church*, the publication of *The New English Hymnal* was surrounded by controversy. In this

---

[1] Ellen M. Leather, 'Carols from Herefordshire' in *Journal of the Folk Song Society*, Vol. iv, No. 14 (June 1910), p. 17. R.V.W. incorporated these extra two verses into his *Fantasia on Christmas Carols* (1912).

case, however, it was the review of the book in *Church Times* that proved controversial.

> The publication in 1906 of *The English Hymnal* is rightly regarded as a landmark in English hymnody. . . . The publication this week of *The New English Hymnal* will be in no sense a landmark. It is not very new; some four hundred of its five hundred hymns come from the earlier book, and three quarters of the remainder have been tried out in *English Praise*. The editors regard most post-war hymnody as 'poor in quality and ephemeral in expression'. Consequently most writers associated with the hymn explosion have scanty representation. . . . Timothy Dudley-Smith is the most favoured of contemporary hymn-writers — apart from George Timms, chairman of the editorial committee. The musicians of the committee contribute considerably to the relatively small number of new tunes. . . . Not much [ousted] from the 1906 collection will be missed, but the book is still 'stuffed out with second-rate creaking translations of Greek and Latin hymns'. . . .[1]

Were these criticisms fair? A reporter at the official launch wrote:

> Apart from the normal hymns — which Mr Timms said were mostly for 'sober and peaceable Anglicans' although some 'popular hymns, typical of the catholic tradition' had slipped in — there is at the end of the book a sizable liturgical section mostly designed for use with the new *Alternative Service Book*. This section includes special words and music for the Church's seasons, feasts and holy days, some plainsong sequences, collects for processions and psalms. It also includes a new English Folk Mass for Rite A, well suited to congregational participation.[2]

A setting of Rite B to Merbecke has also been included. The psalms are by Dom Gregory Murray, most already having appeared in *English Praise*. As in *Ancient and Modern New Standard*, several of the hymns have been transposed down.

---

[1] [Canon] Alan Dunstan, 'Not-so-radical revision' in *Church Times*, 6415 (24 January 1986), p. 5.

[2] Claire Disbrey, 'Revised hymnal for "sober and peaceable Anglicans"' in *Church of England Newspaper*, 4784 (31 January 1986), p. 16.

There was a considerable amount of subsequent correspondence.

> I was disturbed by Canon Dunstan's damning review. . . . A reviewer must be free to criticise, but his criticisms must be tempered by an attitude which is basically benevolent — especially so in the case of a new hymn-book published after many years of hard work. . . . The book is a revision, not a new hymnal. . . . I consider [it] to be an excellent piece of work. The brilliance of the original has been conserved; omissions and blemishes have been corrected; new tunes have been added. I look forward to using it at Southwark Cathedral.[1]

However, the rejection of 'anything broadly charismatic' was regretted by a Director of Ordinands:

> It is true that the erudite . . . can easily point to examples of the naive and the simplistic within the Renewal Movement. I do find it worthy of comment, though, that . . . it is our Sunday evening praise service, where these charges could most easily be levelled, to which hundreds of (mainly young) people come flocking. In this we are not unique. Like many priests my natural sympathies lie with the preservation of a high musical standard in worship, . . . but the charismatic Renewal Movement challenges this. The Church of England cannot ignore this.[2]

This seems a valid point, however difficult we may find it, but the reply from Archdeacon Timms seemed antagonistic:

> I am uncertain of the precise meaning of the term 'charismatic' as used in current Christian parlance and would value enlightenment. . . . In my understanding of the term, *any* good hymn is charismatic — or it is not a good hymn. . . . I am told that 'choruses' (whatever they are) are a sign of the charismatic. Certainly there are plenty of hymns . . . which have a refrain after each verse which could be sung with gusto. . . . We have included 'Were you there?' and 'Lord of the Dance' and 'Living Lord'. Are they

---

[1] Harry Bramma '*The New English Hymnal*' in *Church Times*, 6418 (14 February 1986), p. 14.

[2] [Canon] Michael Banks, 'Hymns and renewal' in *Church Times*, 6417 (2 February 1986), p. 15.

accounted 'broadly charismatic'? We did indeed reject that curious American folksong which appears in recent hymnals, 'Let us break bread together on our knees'[1] — which, to an Anglican at least, would be an extraordinary proceeding.[2]

A fuller explanation of the thinking behind *The New English Hymnal* eventually appeared.[3] Another reviewer at its official launch felt that 'at times drama and emotional intensity [had] been sacrificed to respectability', but that this was 'the best book for those who want traditional liturgy'.[4] In lighter vein, he wondered what Vaughan Williams would have thought of the obliteration of the Dorian mode in 'Greensleeves', and drew attention to the misprint in 'All glory, laud and honour', and its doctrinal implications:

> Though art the King of Israel,
> Thou David's royal Son . . .

Both *The New English Hymnal* and *Hymns Ancient and Modern New Standard* are now published by the Canterbury Press at Norwich. Oxford University Press, publisher of *The English Hymnal*, was approached in the mid-1970s concerning the production of a new book, but the price quoted was felt to be too high. Hymns Ancient and Modern Ltd offered a lower price, which was accepted.[5] (The 1933 edition will continue to be published by OUP for the foreseeable future.)

Although I am aware of no long-term plan for the ultimate merger of these two old rivals, the original aim of the compilers of *The English Hymnal* was for it to be merely a supplement to *Hymns Ancient and Modern*. Now that they share a common publisher, is it possible that this will be the

[1] For example in *Hymns Ancient and Modern New Standard*.
[2] G.B. Timms, 'Charismatic element in *The New English Hymnal*' in *Church Times*, 6418 (14 February 1986), p. 14.
[3] George Timms, 'Hymns for Today's Anglicans' in *Church Music Quarterly*, July 1992, pp. 22–23.
[4] Martyn Cundy, '500 well-loved English hymns' in *Church of England Newspaper*, 4789 (7 March 1986), p. 6.
[5] Marianne Barton, 'From Ancient to Modern' in *Church Music Quarterly*, April 1990, pp. 16–17.

next development, or will the two 'markets' be sufficiently diverse to justify continuation of two separate publications? Alternatively, a 'core' book could cover the common ground, with a choice of supplements. If, however, the ordination of women to the priesthood creates a schism within the Church of England, it is possible that those departing will require their own hymn book.

In addition to the 'mainstream' Anglican hymnals, many interdenominational books are in fairly widespread use in the Church of England. Virtually all these have been published or republished in the last twenty years.[1] We briefly look at these, in chronological order of the date of publication (or, where applicable, that of the parent volume).

The *Public School Hymn Book* was first published in 1903. If not strictly Anglican, it nonetheless had a strong Anglican flavour. While it obviously was directed towards a very specialised group, within that group it was very successful, and revised editions appeared in 1919 and 1949. A total revision of the book in the early 1960s resulted in a change of name to *Hymns for Church and School*.[2] Long describes the book as excellent, 'representative of all periods and particularly rich in twentieth-century hymns and tunes'.[3] Its supplement *Praise and Thanksgiving*[4] contains hymns written in the twenty years since the previous book, as well as some older ones. Its preface states that the aim was to 'combine high artistic standards with *singability* so that hymns may be sung and enjoyed, and remembered with pleasure and profit'. Its launch by the Headmasters' Confer-

---

[1] Also, each of the other major denominations has its own hymnal and, of these, several have produced a supplement and/or new edition in recent years or are in the process of planning one. These books, however, in general fall outside the scope of the present work (although in a few instances they are used by Anglicans, for example in ecumenical churches).

[2] *Hymns for Church and School* (Headmasters' Conference, Henley-on-Thames, 1964).

[3] Kenneth R. Long, *The Music of the English Church* (Hodder and Stoughton, London, 1972), p. 401.

[4] *Praise and Thanksgiving* (Headmasters' Conference, Henley-on-Thames, 1985).

ence at Radley College prompted a vicar's wife to question the need for such a hymn book:

> It is continuing the divisiveness that public schools are at such pains to end — or are they? It was Jilly Cooper who said that the upper classes went to church to have a 'jolly good sing', and I suspect that this is what this new book is all about. . . . This should be a time for uniting people with one or two good hymnbooks sung by all congregations; and I am sorry that public schools in particular should issue their 'own' book.[1]

Songs of Praise[2] was conceived as a hymnal national rather than denominational in character. For almost half a century it was widely used in schools. As can be seen from the preface, the book was a reaction against Victoriana:

> Our churches, both Anglican and Free Church, have alienated during the last half-century much of the strongest character and intelligence of the Nation by the use of weak verse and music.

Inevitably such reactions can be taken to excess, and Long[3] described the book as being 'aggressively typical of the 1920s'. Although still in print, it is little used nowadays.

In the 1960s the BBC launched a programme called 'Songs of Praise', a television version of its long-established radio 'Sunday Half Hour' of congregational hymn-singing. To celebrate the 21st anniversary of 'Songs of Praise' a hymn-writing competition was organised. From 500 entries, fifteen were chosen and published under the title *New Songs of Praise 1*[4].

The *BBC Hymn Book*[5] was compiled so that listeners to such programmes as 'The Daily Service' might follow the

---

[1] Mary-June Scott, 'Divisive new hymnbook' in *Church Times*, 6381 (31 May 1985) p. 13.

[2] (a) *Songs of Praise* (OUP, London, 1925); (b) *Songs of Praise (Enlarged Edition)* (OUP, London, 1931).

[3] Long, p. 401.

[4] *New Songs of Praise 1* (OUP, Oxford, 1986). Volumes 2–6 have more recently been published.

[5] *BBC Hymn Book* (OUP, London, 1951).

words. As might be expected, in due course a supplementary
volume, *Broadcast Praise*, appeared.[1] Neither book has ever
been widely used in churches. The BBC also publishes
school hymnals: two million copies of *Come and Praise 1*[2],
were sold in its first ten years. *Come and Praise 2*,[3] 'the
first anthology to reflect the "broadly Christian" emphasis of
worship outlined in the 1988 Education Reform Act'[4], was
then published. The event provided the background for a
situation which, though trivial in itself, illustrates the deep
feelings which any controversy in church music can so
easily cause. A letter appeared in *Church Times*[5] deploring
the inclusion of the following hymn in the book:

> You can weigh an elephant's auntie,
> You can weigh a pedigree flea,
> But you can't weigh up all the love,
> That Jesus has for me, me, me,
> That Jesus has for me.

Next week there appeared an official denial[6] from the
book's editor that the hymn was in *Come and Praise 2* at
all. The following week the author explained[7] that the hymn
had begun its life in a primary school assembly, and that it
had indeed been published, but in *New Songs of Praise 4*.[8]
A week later, the following news item appeared:

> That elephant's auntie certainly caught the imagination of our
> readers. . . . Nothing — apart from the ordination of women priests
> — has brought so many letters in recent years. The regrettable

1 *Broadcast Praise* (OUP, Oxford, 1981).
2 *Come and Praise 1* (BBC, London, 1978).
3 *Come and Praise 2* (BBC, London, 1989).
4 'BBC school hymnbook already a sell-out' in *Church Times*, 6569 (6 January
   1989), p. 2.
5 John Ewington, 'Rubbish in Song' in *Church Times*, 6570 (13 January 1989),
   p. 14.
6 Geoff Marshall, 'Hymn *not* in new book' in *Church Times*, (20 January
   1989), p. 12.
7 C.J. Brown, 'Hymn defended by author' in *Church Times*, 6572 (27 January
   1989), p. 12.
8 *New Songs of Praise 4* (OUP, Oxford, 1988).

thing is that . . . because the hymn is *not* in the new BBC hymn-book for schools, [the letters] never saw the light of day. . . . Although there were those who thought [the] hymn was 'rubbish' and a blot on the escutcheon of church music, there were plenty more who got the message — that you can't weigh up all the love that Jesus has for me.[1]

Youth Praise 1[2] can be seen as the forerunner of the new, less formal type of Christian music. Its editor, Michael Baughen, later went on to be consultant editor of *Hymns for Today's Church*, and subsequently Bishop of Chester. In the preface he wrote: 'This book has been compiled to try to meet the evident need for a composite youth music book in Christian youth groups of many kinds.' Many of the 150 items had been published elsewhere, notably in Church Special Service Mission chorus books, although some were new. The book proved to be extremely popular, with the result that within three years a sequel had been published, this time containing virtually all new material.[3] Leaver has commented on attempts to transfer music of this type into the worship of the local church.

Here they do not work well because their piano and guitar-orientated music for the smaller group cannot carry the weight of the larger congregation. . . . Many of these simple hymns and choruses have worn very thin by constant repetition over the years. Nevertheless it was a timely production and met a need that was being expressed.[4]

The preface to *Sound of Living Waters*[5] proudly proclaims: '[This] is not a collection of songs by "experts"'. It shares with its sequel *Fresh Sounds*[6] some 240 hymns and worship songs, both traditional and contemporary.

---

[1] 'Elephantine' in *Church Times*, 6573 (3 February 1989), p. 10.
[2] *Youth Praise 1* (Falcon, London, 1966).
[3] *Youth Praise 2* (Falcon, London, 1969).
[4] Robin Leaver, *A Hymn Book Survey 1962–80* (Booklet No. 71) (Grove, Nottingham, 1980), p. 16.
[5] *Sound of Living Waters* (Hodder and Stoughton, London, 1974).
[6] *Fresh Sounds* (Hodder and Stoughton, London, 1976).

The music has a simplicity, a gentleness, and a lack of the jingliness associated with CSSM choruses, or the slightly martial air of many of the *Youth Praise* and *Psalm Praise* compositions.[1]

The *Celebration Hymnal*[2] is distinctly Roman in outlook, and as such cannot be regarded as interdenominational in the normal sense of the word. Precisely because of its outlook, however, it is used in some Anglo-Catholic churches. The word 'thorough' must be applied to this work since, with its two volumes plus its 1989 supplement, there are well over 800 items. This effusiveness has resulted in the print being somewhat too small for comfort, certainly in the full-harmony edition. In addition to the hymns, there are some rounds and responsorial material. One of these is 'The Lord has done marvels for me', Gelineau's version of the Magnificat. A line such as:

> He looks on his servant in her nothingness

really comes into the schoolboy-howler category (the words editor of *Hymns for Today's Church* admits that he has a list of such 'gems of hymnody'[3]). Surely the editor of *Celebration Hymnal* should have done something about it: 'lowliness' is after all a tried and tested substitute.

Two thirds of the contents of the original edition of *Hymns Old and New*[4] were taken from *Celebration Hymnal*. However, in due course *Hymns Old and New* (Anglican Edition)[5] appeared, the selection of hymns being based on computer analysis of requests from over 300 parishes. A reviewer[6] commented that the computer must have been very user-friendly to the compilers, for it had selected no

---

[1] Colin Buchanan, *Encountering Charismatic Worship* (Booklet No. 51) (Grove, Nottingham, 1977), p. 18.
[2] *Celebration Hymnal* (Mayhew-McCrimmon, Great Wakering, 1976).
[3] Michael Saward, 'New hymnbook and churchmanship' in *Church Times*, 6253 (17 December 1982), p. 12.
[4] *Hymns Old and New* (Mayhew, Leigh-on-Sea, 1979).
[5] *Hymns Old and New* (Anglican Edition) (Mayhew, Bury St Edmunds, 1986).
[6] Martyn Cundy, 'Much requested hymns' in *Church of England Newspaper*, 4805 (27 June 1986), p. 7.

fewer than 32 of their own compositions. The book makes no attempt to modernise or feminise the words — were the parishes invited to give their views on this? The reviewer concluded:

> Indisputably, but not aggressively, Anglican, the book is worth serious consideration. It undoubtedly goes a long way towards achieving its aim, to be a unifying hymn-book meeting the needs and tastes of young and old.

With One Voice[1] had already been published two years earlier in Australia as *The Australian Hymn Book*, an ecumenical project with the official backing of five denominations there. After quoting Erik Routley, who described the book as 'just about the most encouraging thing I have seen in the past generation', Leaver writes:

> It may not be trendy . . . but it is certainly not stuffy. . . . I am certain that *With One Voice* is among the best standard hymn books available to churches today.[2]

Sing Alleluia: More Hymns to Sing With One Voice[3] is a supplement of 95 psalms, hymns and spiritual songs. Although the music comes from many lands, and hence is in many styles, Watson[4] has pointed out that the words represent a rather narrow band of Christian experience, in nearly all cases praise and joy of salvation. However, he suggests that the book be examined by all those looking for opportunities to use 'modern hymn' singing to enrich public worship.

In 1980 an innovative project was launched. *Sing Praise*[5] was described as 'the revolutionary new hymn book which allows you to choose exactly what *you* want in it; and you can add to it at any time!' Hymns were purchased on a

---

[1] *With One Voice* (Collins, London, 1979).
[2] Robin Leaver, *A Hymn Book Survey 1962–80* (Booklet No. 71) (Grove, Nottingham, 1980) p. 10.
[3] *Sing Alleluia: More Hymns to Sing With One Voice* (Collins, London, 1987).
[4] Derek Watson, 'Hymns' in *Music in Worship*, 41 (Winter 1988), p. 12.
[5] *Sing Praise* (Kevin Mayhew, Leigh-on-Sea, 1980).

modular basis on individual pages from a menu of over 1,000 items, and then clipped into special binders. All aspects of copyright royalties were handled by the publishers. It was a bold experiment for which, however, the demand was insufficient to make it viable, and the project was eventually abandoned in 1989. Possibly the idea was ahead of its time: we will be looking at copyright on page 55.

Songs of Fellowship Book 1[1] was a compilation of more than 150 recently written worship songs, most of them British. This was followed by *Books 2* and *3*, both with something more of an international flavour. Next was *Hymns of Fellowship*[2], a fairly conventional hymnal but, like the *Songs*, including guitar chords. A combined volume of the four earlier publications, some 650 pieces in all, was produced in 1987.[3] This was followed by *Songs of Fellowship Book 4*,[4] containing some 200 further new songs. In 1991 a volume entitled merely *Songs of Fellowship*[5] was published. This contains a selection of items drawn from earlier editions.[6] The publishers, Kingsway, 'aim to embrace all the worship needs of a growing church'.[7] These include orchestral arrangements and recordings of the songs, recordings of backing tracks for use by a singer when no suitable accompaniment is available, teaching aids for worship, teaching aids for guitarists, and weekend seminars. In addition, there is an annual publication *New Songs*, containing some forty even newer items.

In their introduction to *Jesus Praise*[8], the editors seemed to feel that they should justify the book's existence:

---

[1] *Songs of Fellowship Book 1* (Kingsway, Eastbourne, 1981).
[2] *Hymns of Fellowship* (Kingsway, Eastbourne, 1985).
[3] *Songs and Hymns of Fellowship* (Kingsway, Eastbourne, 1987).
[4] *Songs of Fellowship Book 4* (Kingsway, Eastbourne, 1989).
[5] *Songs of Fellowship* (Kingsway, Eastbourne, 1991).
[6] For some reason or other, the song 'Ain't Jesus Good' has been omitted.
[7] Geoff Shearn, '*Songs of Fellowship* — Much More Than a Songbook' in *Music in Worship*, 36 (July 1986), p. 8.
[8] *Jesus Praise* (Scripture Union, London, 1982).

Revival in the Church has invariably gone hand in hand with musical expression. Hymns, songs, and the shorter, simpler chorus have been pouring out over the past decade. Dozens of song books have been produced all over the world. Why then another? . . . The aim of *Jesus Praise* has been to gather in one book a wide selection of those songs and choruses that have proved their worth over the past years. As well as this, a third of the book contains new and unpublished material.

The editors continued by saying that the book was intended as a replacement for the *Youth Praise* books, but with appeal for adults as well. However, it does not seem to have gained widespread acceptance in worship in the Church of England.

In 1984 the American evangelist Luis Palau visited England to hold a number of large-scale evangelistic meetings under the general title of 'Mission England'. It was felt that no one hymnbook then available seemed entirely suitable for the Mission, and the compilation *Mission Praise*[1] (also published as *Mission England Praise* during the Mission) was born. The book contained an interesting mixture of almost 300 items, hymns old and new together with some revival songs. Margaret Daniel commented that the book was clearly 'not [intending] to break new ground, but to create new enthusiasm'.[2] Archaisms abound. Perhaps significantly the green hill far away is *without* a city wall;[3] while 'Now thank we all our God' uses the traditional tune 'Nun danket' rather than the Beaumont offering of the early sixties. *Mission Praise II* was published in 1987, while *Mission Praise (Combined Edition)*[4] contains both the above books and a supplement, 800 items in all. There is also *Junior Praise*[5], containing 300 songs for children aged 7–11.

---

[1] *Mission Praise* (Marshall, Morgan and Scott, Basingstoke, 1983).
[2] Margaret Daniel, 'Review of *Mission England Praise*' in *Church Times*, 6309 (13 January 1984), p. 6.
[3] See page 33.
[4] *Mission Praise* (Combined Edition) (Marshall Pickering, London, 1990).
[5] *Junior Praise* (Marshall, Morgan and Scott, Basingstoke, 1986).

The first fruits of a further project, encouraging contemporary hymn writers to write on a specific theme, appeared in 1989, entitled *Hymns and Congregational Songs.*[1] A special feature of the project is that photocopying of the material is permitted on a limited basis.

This review of some forty currently available hymnals used in Church of England worship has not been exhaustive. Tremors of the hymn 'explosion' are still being felt, leaving a 'crater' of hymnals in its wake, inevitably with much duplication of hymns between books. Many new worship songs continue to appear, mainly from the Charismatic Movement, but it is likely to be some time before there is another major compilation of material suitable for general Church of England use.

One aim of my survey was to obtain information on the levels of usage of and satisfaction with hymnals. We will be looking at the results of this on page 150.

Next, however, we turn our attention to another type of church-music book, namely the psalter. The Psalms pre-date even the Christian Church by several centuries. In the pre-Reformation Church, and in particular the monastic foundations, the entire psalter was covered each week through its recitation at the seven or eight daily offices. The *Prayer Book* of 1549 reduced this to a monthly cycle in the two daily offices of morning and evening prayer. The greatest change in psalm singing in recent years has been its further reduction, almost to the point of abandonment. This has been caused, at least in part, by the reduced usage of morning and evening prayer, and the widespread substitution of eucharistic services. In Rites A and B of the *ASB*, it is merely specified as an option. The principal of a theological college has gone so far as to say that he believes that the Psalms are dying in the Church of England.[2]

---

[1] *Hymns and Congregational Songs* Vol. 1 No. 1, (Stainer and Bell, London, 1989). Copies are bought direct from the publisher by subscription. Volumes 2 and 3 have now been published.

[2] John Goldingay, 'A store of praise and prayer to reopen' in *Church Times*, 6650 (27 July 1990), p. 8.

The Parish Psalter,[1] edited by Sir Sydney Nicholson, is still quite widely used some sixty years after its publication. It is relatively straightforward to use, but can be very effective in the hands of a competent choir. The *Oxford*[2] and *Worcester*[3] Psalters are somewhat similar to the *Parish*, as they adopt natural speech rhythms. However, they use rather more symbols in their pointing, making them more difficult to use. In less favour are the *Cathedral*[4] and *New Cathedral*.[5] Long describes them respectively as embodying 'the very antithesis of all the principles of good chanting', and 'even worse'.[6]

The Revised Psalter[7] was the work of an Archbishops' Commission, initiated in 1958, to revise the text of the psalter, the first such revision since the Reformation. Indeed the *BCP* version of the psalm texts is essentially that contained in the Coverdale's *Great Bible* of 1539, revised in 1540.

> Although much loved by subsequent generations of Anglicans for its beauty, the Prayer Book Psalter is in effect an English translation of a Latin translation of a Greek translation of the original Hebrew, and consequently not the most accurate rendering of the Psalms.[8]

Dakers has described *The Revised Psalter* as 'a flowing text admirably and simply pointed'[9]. A further and rather more substantial revision appeared only a few years later in the

---

[1] *The Parish Psalter* (Faith Press, Leighton Buzzard, 1928).
[2] *The Oxford Psalter* (OUP, Oxford, 1929).
[3] *The Worcester Psalter* (Adam and Charles Black, London, 1950).
[4] *The Cathedral Psalter* (Novello, London, 1875).
[5] *The New Cathedral Psalter* (Novello, London, 1909).
[6] Kenneth R. Long, *The Music of the English Church* (Hodder and Stoughton, London, 1972), pp. 236, 397.
[7] *The Revised Psalter* (CUP, Eyre and Spottiswoode, OUP and SPCK, London, 1966).
[8] R.C.D. Jasper and Paul F. Bradshaw, *A Companion to the Alternative Service Book* (SPCK, London, 1986), pp. 449–450.
[9] Lionel Dakers, *Church Music at the Crossroads* (Marshall, Morgan and Scott, London, 1970), p. 21.

ASB. These texts and their pointing were also published separately.[1] It will be interesting to see whether the *ASB* translations will last for 450 years, or whether cathedrals will after that time still be using the *BCP* versions. A *Manual of Plainsong*[2] caters for those adopting this alternative method of chanting the psalms, although this practice is rare in parish churches. *BCP* texts are used: I wonder whether *ASB* texts have ever been sung to plainsong.

Recent years have seen the development of other methods of singing the psalms. *Psalm Praise*[3] was the third volume in a series which had produced *Youth Praise 1* and *2*. It included pointed and metrical versions of the canticles, but its chief innovation lay in metrical versions of psalms and other biblical passages.

> Many of the new texts are of a very high quality . . . but the music, with some exceptions is all very much in the same rather superficial style.[4]

A list of alternative tunes was eventually compiled.[5] Another method of singing psalms, originally popularised by the Belgian Jesuit priest Joseph Gelineau, has also been increasingly adopted. It is called the responsorial method, in which a refrain (called an 'antiphon') is sung by the congregation after every two or three verses sung by the choir or cantor. The texts are often taken from the Roman Catholic Grail Psalter.[6] A selection of responsorial psalms has also been included in *The New English Hymnal*.

---

[1] David L. Frost, John A. Emerton and Andrew A. Macintosh, *The Psalms: A New Translation for Worship* (Collins, London, 1977).

[2] H.B. Briggs and W.H. Frere, *A Manual of Plainsong* (Novello, London, 1902); 2nd edn, ed. J.H. Arnold (Novello, London, 1951).

[3] *Psalm Praise* (Falcon, London, 1973).

[4] Robin Leaver, *A Hymn Book Survey 1962–80* (Booklet No. 71) (Grove, Nottingham, 1980), p. 17.

[5] Michael Perry, *Psalm Praise Worship Index* (Falcon, London, 1977).

[6] Publications include: *The Responsorial Psalter, volumes A–C* (Mayhew-McCrimmon, Great Wakering, 1987–1989); *Psalms for Singing* (Mayhew, Bury St Edmunds, 1989); and *Psalms for the Eucharist volumes 1–3* (Mayhew-McCrimmon, Great Wakering, 1984).

Those who are slightly more adventurous, at least in spirit, may well wish to consider the approach adopted at Taizé.[1] Some forty years ago Brother Roger founded the Community of Taizé in the hills of Burgundy, where it now provides a ecumenical retreat from the pressures of the world. The music adviser to the Diocese of Bath and Wells writes:

> The Taizé phenomenon is one that embodies a sense of simplicity and authenticity in worship, together with flexibility and freedom of prayer and music. Add to this the international flavour of the thousands of people who flock there each year, and you will have some idea of its universal appeal.
>
> The ever increasing range of Taizé music is becoming more and more well known as songs are brought back by those who go there, and as the Brothers themselves visit the poor and deprived in all parts of the world. . . . Whether used in small or large groups, the music of Taizé is compelling and haunting. Some of the more contemplative refrains [antiphons] can be used in smaller churches during Communion services, like 'O Lord hear my prayer' [*Psalm 102*].[2]

Methods of psalm singing are discussed in more detail elsewhere[3].

Books of the Future

The duplication of hymns and settings of psalms between different books is clearly wasteful both in paper and expense, but seems unavoidable for the foreseeable future. At many churches where congregational music is drawn from a number of different books, loose-leaf compilations have been produced. However, the question of copyright on even one hymn can be far from straightforward, and when multiplied several times over becomes a formidable task. Regrettably but not altogether surprisingly, many churches

---

[1] For example, *Psalms from Taizé* (Mowbray, London, 1983).

[2] John Newman, 'The Music of Taizé' in *Christian Music*, Autumn 1989, pp. 10–11.

[3] Robin Leaver, David Mann and David Parkes, *Ways of Singing the Psalms* (Collins, London, 1985).

have succumbed to the temptation to ignore the copyright laws altogether. A central clearing-house on hymn copyright has for some time been advocated.[1] In a sense this was precisely what the *Sing Praise* project was trying to achieve. Possibly its ultimate downfall lay in the fact that potential subscribers were seeking a larger selection of hymns than those for which the proprietors could readily obtain copyright permission. A leaflet explaining, amongst other things, the legalities of making local hymnbooks has been published by the Pratt Green Trust.[2] The Trust offers assistance in tracing copyright holders, but is not in any way the clearing house that is so badly needed. However, the Christian Music Association (formerly the Christian Music Publishers' Association) has been operating such a scheme.[3] In 1991 responsibility for the scheme was transferred to Christian Copyright Licensing UK Ltd. It is understood that more than 400 publishers are now participating in the scheme.

In addition to the trend from bound hymnbooks to loose-leaf compilations, made easy (technically at least) by photocopying, technology has been opening other horizons. Overhead projectors can in principle dispense with paper books altogether: slides of *Songs of Fellowship* words are available from the publishers. Indeed the words can now even be loaded into a church's microcomputer, for display to the congregation.[4]

It seems unimaginable that the conventionally printed hymnal will ever be supplanted. However, technology is developing very quickly indeed, and I would not care to predict the medium in which the next edition of *Hymns Ancient and Modern* will appear.

---

[1] John King, 'Grasping the nettle of hymn copyright' in *Church Times*, 6250 (26 November 1982), p. 10.

[2] *Copyright and the Local Church* (Pratt Green Trust, London, 1989). A new edition is shortly to be published.

[3] 'New copyright scheme' in *Church Times*, 6390 (2 August 1985), p. 2.

[4] Bob Cranham, 'The Writing on the Wall? — Songs of Fellowship OHP System' in *Christian Music*, Winter 1991, pp. 8–9.

Courses and Qualifications

Finally in this chapter, we investigate training courses in church music. Whilst the priest is responsible for the service as a whole and, in particular, the spoken parts, the musical director must bear a major part of the responsibility for the musical element within it. He or she can therefore be termed one of the ministers. What skills are needed for this ministry, and what facilities are available for acquiring them? In the last ten years or so there have been great changes in the courses and qualifications available. Many institutions, of which the best known is the Royal School of Church Music, have involved themselves in this work. Let us first look at the historical background.

In the nineteenth century, cathedral organists accepted pupils, to whom they taught their trade in return for acting as deputies. With the expansion of the universities and music colleges, notably the Royal College of Organists, these apprenticeships gradually became less common. During the present century, the qualifications ARCO and FRCO, and their related choir-master's diploma CHM, have become ever more technically demanding. However, although much of the music in these examinations was composed for sacred use, it has always been studied primarily from a secular viewpoint, without reference to its liturgical context. In this aspect at least, such pupils would be at a disadvantage compared with their nineteenth-century counterparts. If this was all the training that was available to the professionals during the first part of this century, certainly the amateur musicians in the parishes could not reasonably hope for anything better.

Since 1929 the Royal School of Church Music (or, as it then was, the School of English Church Music) has been actively involved in the training of church musicians. Apart from occasional visits of a Commissioner to affiliated choirs, until 1974 this training was primarily aimed at a professional level, with courses of up to a year's duration. Most students prepared for the diplomas of the Royal College of Organists but, in the words of the Prospectus, they were also given 'the opportunity to study the art of public worship, with particular reference to the part played in it by music'.

Since 1974 the RSCM's work has been much more directed towards the amateur, through its many diverse short residential and one-day courses at Addington Palace in Croydon, and 'on site' through the expertise of its travelling Commissioners.[1]

One of the RSCM's responsibilities is the administration of the Archbishop of Canterbury's Diploma in Church Music.

> The Anglican church felt that skill in organ-playing and choir-training, though essential, did not go far enough and that church musicians needed further training in such specialised studies as liturgiology, Prayer Book history, plainsong, Anglican chanting and pointing, hymnody, and similar specialist fields. Such training would help bridge the gap between clergy and their organists. To meet this need Archbishop Lang instituted in 1937 a new examination, the Archbishop of Canterbury's Diploma in Church Music (ADCM), which involves a wide course of study embracing subjects unheard of by the old articled pupils [of cathedral organists] — or their masters. Just as entry for the choir-training diploma is restricted to holders of one of the RCO organ diplomas, so for the ADCM examination only those are eligible who hold both the FRCO and CHM diplomas.[2]

The limitations of the ADCM are threefold. Firstly, the number of successful candidates (one or two per year) is too small for the qualification to be widely known. Secondly, and this may be the cause of the first, there is at present no specific course of training for the qualification. Finally, both in name and content it is based on the Anglican Church. The RSCM also awards three types of honorary diploma (associateship, honorary membership, and fellowship) and is considering the introduction of some new examination,

---

[1] Bryan Anderson, 'Seven whole days, not one in seven' in *Church Music Quarterly*, January 1992, pp. 18–19.

[2] Kenneth R. Long, *The Music of the English Church* (Hodder and Stoughton, London, 1972), p. 393.

either on its own or in collaboration with some other institution.

In 1991 the Christian Musicians' and Artists' Trust took over half of the responsibilities of the former Christian Music Association.[1] The Trust is seeking through its Personal Membership scheme:

> . . . to provide an infrastructure that will facilitate the linking of all Christians who have a specific interest in worship, Christian music and related arts. . . [including] musicians, singers, dancers, worship leaders, church leaders, songwriters, organisers of music events, technicians and publishers.

The newest of the bodies involved with courses and qualifications is CHIME (the Churches' Initiative in Music Education).

> CHIME began when a working party, called together (by the RSCM) to investigate the potential for qualifications in church music, heard . . . about the philosophy behind the recent revision of the [Archbishops' Certificate in Church Music — page 61]. This, together with news of similar revisions of examination syllabuses etc, by the Royal College of Organists and others, coincided with a presentation from [Prof.] Bob Reeve, of Anglia Polytechnic, on the opportunities within the Credit Accumulation and Transfer systems now being introduced throughout Europe. He concluded his talk with a suggestion that the various church music organisations should meet to investigate the possibilities of co-ordinating and evaluating the training and qualifications currently available. We decided to expand our working party so as to take in as many shades of opinion and churchmanship as possible. . . .
>
> CHIME should be careful to gain academic and ecclesiastical support and credibility: if CHIME is to be a useful forum, perhaps even a co-ordinating and commissioning body, then its every movement will need to be in tune with the local and national church's needs. Having met and talked with those involved so far, I am happy to report some fascinating glimpses of potential harmony. . . .[2]

---

[1] The other responsibilities were transferred to Christian Copyright Licensing Ltd. (page 56).

[2] Geoff Twigg, 'CHIME' in *Laudate*, 17 (Spring 1991), pp. 4–6.

In 1981 the City of Liverpool College of Higher Education introduced a Music and Worship course leading to a BA honours degree of the University of Lancaster, the first such course in Britain leading to a degree. Teaching was shared between the Departments of Music and Religious Studies, drawing also on the resources of both the Anglican and Metropolitan cathedrals, and many other Merseyside churches. The course was widely publicised to attract the target student intake of 24 although, in 1981, only nine students began. The following year's intake was down to four, caused by absence of publicity, the sudden death of the course's founder Gerald Brown, and financial pressure upon the college (ultimately leading to its merger with Liverpool Polytechnic). During the year 1982/83 it was decided to discontinue the course. Of the thirteen students, nine graduated.

Since 1981, the BA honours degree at Colchester Institute[1] has been offering Christian Liturgical Music as a major option in its second and third years, comprising 40% of the entire degree. The option covers three areas: liturgical tradition (history of church music to the present day), placement (two years in a church of the student's denomination), and composition. Students are encouraged to attend each other's services from time to time, so that they may respect their colleagues' differing traditions and broaden their own experience. The course produces roughly five graduates per year. The head of the School of Music has written:

> What we are *not* about is 'musicians who live in organ lofts'. We pride ourselves on being actively concerned with music for the people of God, not for the musically elite. However, our BA syllabus as such can cope with the needs of those who want to take ARCO/FRCO or whatever, but our first concern is the management and performance of music at a pastoral level.[2]

---

[1] Now an Associate College of Anglia Polytechnic which, in turn, will shortly become Anglia Polytechnic University.

[2] William Tamblyn, 'Liturgical music' in *Church Times*, 6623 (19 January 1990), p. 13.

The Faculty of Church Music was founded in 1956 as an interdenominational body promoting church music. It offers examinations at three levels: associate, licentiate and fellow. Alternative options to organ playing or singing include composition and choir training.

Since its foundation in 1888, the Guild of Church Musicians has undergone two changes of name, first from 'The Church Choir Guild' to 'The Incorporated Guild of Church Musicians' and, in recent years, to its present name. The Guild has some 600 members. In addition to the *Year Book*, there is a quarterly magazine *Laudate*. It also holds an annual one-day conference, embracing the annual general meeting. In 1961, Archbishop Fisher gave to the Guild the charge of administering a new examination — the Archbishop of Canterbury's Certificate in Church Music, ACertCM. Initially the practical part of this examination was for organists and choirmasters only but, is now open to singers and cantors as well. The syllabus was revised in 1987 to enable Roman Catholics to take the examination. At that time, Cardinal Basil Hume Archbishop of Westminster became, with the Archbishop of Canterbury, joint Patron of the Guild, and the examination's title was changed to the Archbishops' Certificate in Church Music. For whom is it intended? The Guild's prospectus reads:

> It is the expressed hope of the Archbishops that all who have the responsibility of leading the music of their church should aim to achieve the Certificate as a basic, minimum acceptable standard of music coupled with an understanding of the forms of service in which they exercise their special ministry.

Much has been done to publicise the examination and to assist candidates to take it. There are evening classes being run in different parts of the country, residential training weekends (with grants available from the Leverhulme Trust), and there is now even a correspondence course. There are rewards for those who pass the examination, such as the letters ACertCM (recognised as a valid qualification by the Incorporated Society of Musicians), and an academic hood.

All these have had an effect in arousing interest but, with less than 300 Certificates awarded in the first thirty years, the words of the Archbishops cannot be seen as anything more than what might be termed a pious hope for some considerable time to come. However, recent changes in the syllabus and the creation of an academic board may well play their part in improving the situation. Since 1985 the Guild has also offered an advanced diploma course, intermediate in difficulty between ACertCM and ADCM: this too will probably take a number of years to become established.

The Music in Worship Trust was founded in 1984 by a small group of organists wishing to become more involved in the worshipping community. It has recently changed its name to the Music and Worship Foundation. It organises church-music workshops, and in 1991 initiated a one-year regional training programme. In collaboration with the London Bible College, it is proposing to begin a more formal one-year course and, eventually, a combined degree course in theology and church music. It is closely associated with the quarterly magazine *Christian Music* (*Music in Worship* until 1987). In an interview, director Robin Sheldon summarised the aims:

> [We try] to offer help and advice to all churches, across the whole range of what's available for instruments and voices, as to how best to use music in worship; and to look at the role it should occupy in this context. . . . I know as a musician how important it is to deal with the nuts and bolts of performance, but it remains a tool in worship, not a tool to praise music.[1]

Although MWF might appear to be in competition with the activities of the RSCM (and indeed some of its members may at one time have wished it to be), there is now a large measure of co-operation between the two bodies.

In 1987 the Royal Academy of Music introduced a Church Music course as part of its Complementary Studies pro-

---

[1] John Greenhalgh, 'Music in Worship Trust' in *Church Times*, 6620 (29 December 1989), p. 15.

gramme. It is run in co-operation with St. Marylebone Parish Church and the RSCM. Lecturers include the clergy and organists of a number of cathedrals, both Anglican and Roman: observation visits to those cathedrals comprise a significant part of the course. All students must first win their place at the Academy in their principal study (instrument or voice). The course may be taken as a one-year major option either by postgraduate students, or by those preparing for, or pre-elected to, a university organ scholarship. Other students (Performers, GRSM or BMus) can take different parts of the course throughout their three or four years spent at the Academy. The course generally has twelve regular students per year of whom, on average, all but one will be Anglicans (the exception normally being Roman Catholic), and of whom nine will be organists and three singers. The director of the course has indicated the reasons for launching it.

> This country's musical traditions have grown directly out of the rich soil of its diverse church music. But, over the last 20 years, liturgical practices and attitudes to music in worship have changed and developed at a rate unknown for generations, subjecting church musicians to new challenges and imperatives. The Academy's new course is intended as a positive response. . . .
>
> [The] course must extend its reach across denominational barriers, while maintaining a keen appreciation of denominational traditions. Second, it has to lay equal stress on purely musical skills and the understanding needed for their sensitive and imaginative application, an understanding involving aspects of liturgy, theology, pastoral care and administration. This philosophy ensures the course will convey the essentially 'ministerial' nature of the church musician's work.[1]

As an expression of his concern at the poor state of music in cathedrals in the first half of the nineteenth century, the Revd Sir Frederick Gore Ouseley in 1856 founded the

---

[1] Patrick Russill, 'Training Tomorrow's Church Musicians' in *Church Music Quarterly*, April 1990, p. 19.

College of St Michael at Tenbury Wells in Worcestershire, the first new choral foundation since the Reformation.

> It was intended to serve as a model to the whole Church in the efficient rendering of daily choral services, in the selection of a truly representative repertoire of the best sacred music, and in the well-ordered education of choirboys under ideal conditions. Its very existence challenged the slackness everywhere else. . . . There are now seven lay clerks and the school has been expanded to take seventy boys, of whom eighteen are on the choral foundation.[1]

St Michael's Tenbury is no more. In 1985 the number of pupils had fallen below 50, making the College no longer financially viable. It closed in July of that year. The decline in pupils was blamed on the fact that the College was set in a sparsely populated catchment area, and plans to move to another area proved to be either unsuitable or incompatible with the founder's intention.[2] However, some felt that the College might have been saved, had the trustees alerted the public to the problems earlier.[3]

A new MMus course in English Church Music has recently been introduced by the School of Art History and Music at the University of East Anglia. This is the first higher-degree course in church music in Britain, and is being taught in collaboration with the organist of Norwich Cathedral. The course includes tuition in composition, performance (organ or singing), and choir training and conducting, as well as the preparation of a 10,000-word dissertation on some aspect of the history of English church music. The course has a considerably higher music content and correspondingly lower liturgical content than those at Colchester and the Academy.

---

[1] Kenneth R. Long, *The Music of the English Church* (Hodder and Stoughton, London, 1972), pp. 324–5.

[2] 'Top choir school to close soon' in *Church Times*, 6372 (29 March 1985), p. 3.

[3] Julian W.S. Litten, 'Closure of a college' in *Church Times*, 6377 (3 May 1985), p. 13.

In 1983 there appeared an advertisement stating that, from October that year, the University of St Andrews would be offering a one-year postgraduate diploma in church music.[1] The teaching was to be shared between the Department of Music and the Faculty of Divinity. The only student took the course in 1985/6, the first year of operation. The diploma ended when the Department of Music was reduced in 1988.

The Williams School of Church Music, situated in Harpenden, Hertfordshire, became an independent institution with charitable status in 1971, although it had been a privately owned school for some ten years previously. It served two distinct but complementary needs. On the one hand, it was a conventional preparatory school, but one which provided specialist training for prospective cathedral choristers. On the other, it held training courses for adult church musicians, both through evening classes and by correspondence. This led to the award of a diploma and, after further study, to associateship of the college. Roughly twenty students per year reached this level. The school finally closed its doors seven years ago, the victim of financial difficulties.

To summarise, the number of courses in the 'professional' category is expanding, those already well established being those at Colchester Institute and the Royal Academy of Music. The latter is not, as yet, a first study (with no qualification being awarded), but this is understood to be under consideration. Whilst the Academy's list of lectures and activities may be the more impressive, the course director[2] admits that this is at the cost of a 'living and regular liturgical focal point for "hands-on" experience', an essential part of the Colchester course. It is perhaps significant that the directors of both the Colchester and Academy courses are Roman Catholics, rather than Anglicans as might have been expected. A further important point is that, compared with the number of those required to exercise musical leadership in some capacity in the Church today, the

---

[1] For example in *Church Times*, 6281 (1 July 1983), p. 16.

[2] Patrick Russill, 'Training Tomorrow's Church Musicians' in *Church Music Quarterly* (April 1990) p. 19.

number of those with any formal training specifically in church music must be regarded as extremely small.

My questionnaire survey investigates the musical training (or rather the lack of it) offered to theological students. However, it may be noted at this stage that, apart from the proposed partnership of the Music and Worship Foundation and London Bible College, there is nothing in Britain comparable to either the four-year Bible and Music Programme at the European Bible Institute at Lamorlaye, France[1], or the one-year Master of Divinity with Church Music degree at the South Eastern Baptist Theological Seminary at Wake Fort, East Carolina. In particular, the syllabus of the Master of Ministry degree course, introduced in 1990 at the University of Sheffield, does not cover the use of music in worship at all.

The following extract from the submission of the Royal College of Organists to the recent Archbishops' Commission on Church Music provides a fitting close to this chapter:

> There is a profound need for more practical musical training and liturgical education among clergy and organists respectively. This should be tackled particularly at the student level. The College stands ready to discuss and promote new initiatives, and believes that the theological colleges should examine and improve their courses in respect of music radically. At the same time it is hoped that the theological colleges themselves could provide 'short' courses for church musicians. There should be open and constructive discussions, formally constituted, aimed at producing future generations of musically trained and liturgically educated musicians and clergy. This way lies the route to high quality work and lack of mutual suspicion between the two groups.[2]

[1] Susanne Slack, 'Training for Music Ministry' in *Christian Music*, Spring 1990, pp. 20–23.

[2] 'Archbishops' Commission on Church Music' in *Year Book of the Royal College of Organists, 1989–90*, pp. 12–13.

2a

The Call To Arms Is Sounding[1]

Three Case Studies

In this chapter we turn to my survey of church music by means of questionnaire to clergy and church organists. First, however, while the RCO submission emphasising the need for more common ground between the two parties is still fresh in our minds, let us see what can happen when that common ground is missing.

In each of the following true case studies, the principal participants were all well-meaning Christian people. However, their failure to communicate satisfactorily with each other gave rise to great distress — both to themselves and to many who looked to them for leadership. The names of the characters and the churches have of course been changed.

The Sitting Tenant

The Choir Dinner was always such a happy occasion. Each year the PCC voted that St Luke's should show its appreciation of the choir by inviting each adult member and his/her guest to dinner in a local restaurant. The vicar, the church-wardens and their wives always came along too. In his speech, Peter the vicar momentarily forgot exactly how many years Stanley had been organist at the church, and

[1] Mrs Hernaman, [in, for example,] *Hymns Ancient and Modern Standard Edition* (Clowes, London, 1922), No. 583.

stopped to ask him. On being reminded that it was nineteen, he remarked that Stanley's twentieth anniversary would have to be specially commemorated at next year's dinner. Granted, during the rest of the year, Stanley and a few other choir members were known not to get on well with Peter but, at least on this one evening of the year, any differences were forgotten.

Within a month of the dinner, Stanley had been given three months' notice of dismissal and, within a further week, the entire congregation had been split into two warring factions, siding either with Peter or with Stanley. What had brought about this sorry state of affairs, and how did matters subsequently develop?

Stanley had been organist at the church for a long time. A respected head of music at a local school, he felt at ease with upper-middle-of-the-road worship, which is what St Luke's had always offered until this young vicar appeared just six years ago. As soon as he arrived, Peter began to make little changes in the worship and, over the years, the church became gradually more evangelical. Stanley, various members of the choir, and even, it must be said, some members of the congregation were not happy. They felt keenly about this and, although they tried hard, they were unable to get their point of view across to Peter. Oh, how they hated singing choruses! Their only hope was that perhaps they could in time influence the rest of the congregation, who might in turn influence Peter to take things a bit more gently. Perhaps before too long he would be moving on to another church.

But now this terrible news. Stanley had only just got home after taking his wife to hospital, when there was a knock at the door. It was Peter. After passing the time of day, Peter asked him how much longer he intended to stay on as organist at St Luke's, and seemed surprised to learn that Stanley was not intending to leave next year after completing 20 years' service. No, God willing, he intended to stay on for another 20. Then Peter said the fateful words: 'Stanley, I am sorry, but we do not seem to be able to work well together. I must give you three months' notice.' Peter accepted afterwards that he had chosen a very unsuitable occasion on which to discuss the matter with Stanley, and that his off-the-cuff remark at the choir dinner had been most unfortunate. Moreover, he should have consulted the churchwardens before embarking on his present course of action. On the other hand, he knew that Stanley had for years been criticising his ministry, mainly behind his back and, in his shock at realising that Stanley would probably otherwise outlast him, he took the step that he had never before been able to summon up the courage to take.

The criticism of before was nothing compared with the situation on the following Sunday. Battle lines had been drawn. Within a week, the news had been 'leaked' to the local press, and two days later it appeared in the national tabloids. Peter, Stanley, the wardens, even the choir, were involved in long and stressful meetings. Much of the normal work of the church had to be laid aside in order to make time for all these meetings. Then came the visitation from the bishop. Having privately heard the views of those most closely involved, he wanted to learn the consensus of the church. The meeting was very tense and, at its end, the bishop suggested a three-month 'cooling-off' period. This seemed to please no-one since it was felt that all methods of reconciliation had already been tried and had failed. The bishop departed to ponder the matter further.

A week later came the announcement that the bishop had confirmed Peter's decision. Stanley served out his three months' notice and, when he left, half of the choir and about a quarter of the congregation went with him. Some of the congregation eventually returned, but not until after Peter had himself left, a few years later. Stanley felt particularly bitter about the whole affair, the bitterness diminishing only after he had become organist of another church in the same town eighteen months after his dismissal. Peter soon found a new organist who was a keen evangelical. A contract of appointment was drawn up with the assistance of the Royal School of Church Music. This contract was for a period of five years with the possibility of renewal for fixed periods thereafter.

Questions

- How should a vicar deal with the situation of a 'sitting tenant', especially a long-standing one?
- To what extent should he take note of the organist's views on worship, and to what lengths should he go to discover them?
- To what extent should he make an effort to develop a satisfactory working relationship with the organist?
- How important is it that an organist should have a contract of fixed length?
- If a situation becomes intolerable, how should a vicar deal with the matter?

Winds of Change

St Peter's had quite a reputation for its 'bells and smells'. Fr Paul had been vicar there for more than half of his 72 years. Perhaps in a year or so he ought to step aside for someone younger, but there was plenty of time yet. Perhaps the congregation was not as large as it used to be, and there were not many young families, but he understood that other churches were suffering from the same problem and, all in all, things seemed to be ticking over pretty well.

Fr Paul got on very well with Dick his organist, who was in his mid-fifties. Dick was a sales representative, and he had studied for a music diploma in his spare time. Like many amateur musicians, he was immensely keen, and over the last seven years had built up a 20-strong choir of boys and men. These were the days when to make a gramophone record was something rather special, and St Peter's choir had done just that. Moreover the record was selling well throughout the town.

Then Dick had a heart attack, and although he soon recovered sufficiently to return to the console, he felt that he should give notice and retire. This perhaps caused Fr Paul to

consider his own three score years and twelve, because
shortly afterwards it became known that he had gone to see
the bishop about retiring. As he did not want his successor
to arrive at a church with no organist, he immediately
advertised the post. Henry, a musician in his fifties, with an
FRCO and a couple of other diplomas to his name, had
recently taken early retirement and moved into the area. He
was appointed and took up his post six weeks before Fr Paul
finally retired.

Four months later Fr Stephen was inducted as the new
vicar. For the first time in over fifty years the vicarage
reverberated to the sound of a teenage family. His induction
service was magnificent: the augmented choir was well up
to the standard that had been achieved on the record a few
years earlier. Everybody felt that a great new era was about
to begin at St Peter's.

Within a year Henry had resigned. He felt that Fr Stephen
was interfering far too much in the running of the music.
Trying to open membership of the choir to women was just
one example of this interference. For his part, Fr Stephen
regretted that he and Henry had not seen eye to eye: he
would so much have preferred to make the appointment
himself. Henry, he felt, was too set in his ways: Fr Stephen
really wanted someone younger, more in line with his own
ideas.

The post was re-advertised, and this time there was no
applicant. However, it was discovered that a newly-
appointed music teacher at a local girls' school was looking
for accommodation for his wife and young family. The
vicarage was so large that part of it could very easily be
used as a self-contained flat. Thus Bob was appointed.

Fr Stephen's commission from the bishop was to try to
reawaken St Peter's. For as long as anybody could remember, the pattern of worship had always been a said mass at
8.00, a sung mass at 9.30 and evening prayer at 6.30. The
1928 *Prayer Book* had been used at all three services, and
the choir sang at the sung mass and evening prayer. Fr
Stephen felt that there was little chance of the congre-

gation's increasing, as indeed it needed to, with a 1928 eucharist as the main service. He therefore proposed to the PCC that a Rite A service be substituted. This provoked outrage from the PCC, very few of whom had ever attended such a service, and some of whom had no intention of ever doing so.

The only compromise seemed to be a split into two services: a Rite A family mass at 9.30, and a traditional mass at 11.15. The PCC reluctantly agreed to this arrangement. Fr Stephen reconciled himself to the fact that, for the time being, he would have to take three Sunday morning services instead of two, and preach two sermons instead of one (the non-stipendiary minister who had been promised would not be arriving for several months).

The existing all-male choir would sing at the 11.15, whilst Bob would form a new choir of girls from his school to provide music for the less formal 9.30. Any men wishing to sing in both services would be more than welcome to do so. Bob seemed reasonably happy about the arrangement, although it constituted a significant increase in his responsibilities. The men in the choir were less happy. For some, the revised time of 11.15 was difficult, and they transferred to the 9.30 service. Others preferred the traditional type of service, and sang only at the 11.15. Very few sang at both services although, it should be mentioned in passing, there was always a four-part quorum for evensong.

Very few girls could be recruited for the 9.30 service despite Bob's best efforts. The congregation started criticising the girls' lack of volume, and Fr Stephen began to feel that the perfectly adequate choir at the 11.15 should really be there at 9.30 instead. He listened to Bob's misgivings, but in the end overruled them. He was suffering from overwork, and a complaining organist was the last straw. In the resulting transfer to the 9.30 service, the choir lost three men, two of them tenors.

Three months later Bob resigned. This was a difficult decision since it meant finding somewhere else to live, but he could stand it no more. The post of organist now was considerably different from the one he had been offered a year earlier: in particular there was effectively no longer any opportunity to perform traditional liturgical music. Moreover, he felt that decisions relating to music in the church were being taken without adequate reference to him. Fr Stephen was very sorry that Bob felt like this: it was so unfortunate that he had been appointed during a phase of transition within the church.

The post was advertised, but there was no applicant. It was advertised more widely, and again no response. During the interregnum, Phil — a member of the congregation, and a music teacher at another local school, but in no real sense of the word an organist — had volunteered to run things. Fr Stephen gladly grasped this lifeline, but the men in the choir were less happy. They felt that Phil used to treat them as though they were in his class at school, and this reached a climax on one occasion when he could not attend evensong because of a school concert. One of the longer-serving members of the choir, although not really a keyboard player, had agreed to play the organ. Since Phil's arrival, no anthem had been sung at evensong despite the vocal resources being available, and several members of the choir agreed that it would be good to sing a short unaccompanied anthem, like old times. Fr Stephen was only too happy to agree, and the anthem was duly sung. When Phil got to hear of this, he said he felt that the choir had been disloyal to him, and that the choir was not in future going to be allowed to attend evensong at all. Fr Stephen was appalled at this, but since Phil was threatening to resign over the matter, and since there was no-one else both willing and able to play on a regular basis, he felt obliged to go along with it.

Phil stayed at the church for some further time before moving on to another teaching appointment elsewhere. During this time, the choir gradually collapsed, partly because there was not enough for it to do: as members left, their places were not filled.

Questions

• Was Fr Paul acting in the best interests of his successor, and of the church, when he appointed Henry?
• Were the resignations of Henry or Bob to the benefit of the church? If not, to what extent should efforts have been made to persuade them to stay?
• If they had been on the PCC, might their resignations have been averted?
• Ought Fr Stephen to have stood his ground at Phil's ultimatum, even at the risk of losing his third organist within two years of his arrival at the church?

Chalk and Cheese

All seemed settled at St George's, a large church in the centre of a moderate-sized town. Roger had been organist for ten years, and Martin vicar for five. Roger had been a choirboy at the church many years earlier, and in his teens had been taught the organ up to Grade 8 by the then organist. When the organist retired, Roger seemed the natural successor. There had always been a flourishing choir which sang a choral setting at the morning eucharist, and an anthem at evensong each week. Now, however, owing to relocation of Roger's work, St George's was having to look for a new organist. Of all the candidates, Nigel was by far the most promising. He was in his forties, held several music diplomas, and did much freelance playing and teaching. Martin, the vicar, saw in Nigel someone who could assist his own plans for really putting St George's on the map. They were roughly the same age, which also seemed promising. There was only one problem. Nigel was one of the Associated Board's overseas examiners, and consequently would be unavailable for two months each summer.

Martin did not have to wait long before Nigel's energies began to have an effect. He soon persuaded the PCC to create the post of organ scholar, open to a music student at the local university. This post was soon filled by James, who would play the organ while Nigel conducted the choir. The standard of the choir began to rise, and this in turn encouraged others to join, in some cases from quite far afield. In addition to the 90-minute Friday practice, there was now a 30-minute warm-up before both of the Sunday services. The carol service was the best that anyone could remember. Although Martin had earlier thought that Nigel was possibly over-qualified, he was now confident that the right choice had been made.

As the choir continued to improve, so its repertoire increased. Each week it would now sing one or two motets at the eucharist, and an introit and an anthem at evensong. For a time there was a fully choral evensong on one Sunday each month but, after adverse comments were received from members of the congregation, this was changed to a Saturday evening. Each week the choir continued to sing an introit and anthem at Sunday evensong. Superimposed on this were a number of choral weddings, fund-raising concerts for the church, and the occasional choral service on weekday evenings. Nigel also instituted a series of lunchtime organ recitals for office workers.

Although Martin and Nigel seemed to get on well together, one or two things about each of them got on the other's nerves. For his part, after processing in, Martin always wanted the organ music to stop as soon as he arrived in the stalls. On several occasions he spoke loudly into the microphone without giving whoever was playing the chance to finish. This irritated both Nigel and James. On the other hand, Nigel liked to conduct the choir from *decani* side, while the organ console was on *cantoris*. However, since Nigel felt James to be incapable of playing certain pieces — a view which many felt to be as inaccurate as it was frequent — he was often moving to and fro across the chancel during the service. Both Martin and the congregation found this very distracting. As the tensions were building up between Martin and Nigel, the latter began one of his overseas examining tours. On his return, he learned that Martin had been advised by his doctor to take life a little easier. Their meetings became less and less frequent, and arrangements were increasingly made by telephone and correspondence. Another issue that divided the two men was the question of choral services during the month of August. Nigel argued that, since the choir was working hard during the rest of the year, it deserved a break. However, Martin felt that it should be possible to maintain some sort of four-part quorum, especially since so many tourists normally attended the services in August.

Four years after being appointed, Nigel resigned. He felt that for three of them Martin had not been at all co-operative. In addition, the salary had not been increasing in line with the rates recommended by the Royal School of Church Music. On those occasions when James was also absent, Nigel was having to pay a deputy out of his own pocket at a higher rate than he was receiving. For his part, Martin felt that, although both he and Nigel had been wanting the musical standard to be built up, Nigel had been trying to create a cathedral choir in a parish church. In some ways he was sorry to see Nigel go, but he felt that perhaps someone else might be more suitable. James felt that the two men were too strong-willed to be able to work with each other. Each had his own vision for the church, and unfortunately these visions had not coincided. The combination of three months' notice from Nigel and James's remaining time as organ scholar gave Martin six months in which to find a new organist. Almost immediately an advertisement was placed in *Church Times*, but none of the applicants was remotely suitable. After this, nothing further happened until after James had left, whereupon the post was readvertised. At that time, several members of the choir left to join other choirs, including a secular one recently founded by Nigel.

The applications to the second advertisement were more promising, including one from an assistant organist at a cathedral. He was offered the appointment but, as he was unable to find a suitable teaching appointment, he had to decline. The second choice was Kenneth, another professional musician. Although his home and work were both 40 miles away, he felt confident that, if he took the appointment, the commuting would not be an undue problem until such time as he could move to the area. Since none of the other candidates was at all suitable, Kenneth was appointed. The post of organ scholar fell into abeyance. Very soon Kenneth came to realise that the travel did pose a serious problem and, when he discovered the price of houses within a ten-mile radius of St George's, realised that he could not afford to move. All his salary as organist (still below the level recommended by the RSCM) was being spent in travel. Being away from home all day each Sunday was most unsatisfactory, and he found that he was lacking both the enthusiasm and the energy to embark on a recruiting drive to fill the now quite empty choir stalls. Within a year of his appointment, he resigned.

After considerable further advertising, Bill was appointed. Bill's vision was to reintroduce an all-male choir at St George's after a break of 20 years. In mentioning this to the sopranos he suggested that their presence might possibly be an inhibiting factor in recruiting boys. The sopranos took the hint: some contraltos did not even wait to be asked.

Questions

- In the light of subsequent events, was Martin wrong in appointing Nigel?
- Given the fact that Martin and Nigel were such strong personalities, could the collision course have reasonably been foreseen and even avoided? If so, how?
- Is there any means by which a vicar and a potential organist can discover whether they will be able to work satisfactorily together? If so, what?
- In the light of subsequent events, was Martin wrong in appointing Kenneth?
- What is the likelihood of Bill successfully re-introducing an all-male choir? Laying musical considerations aside, what are the pastoral advantages and disadvantages of such a plan?

2b

Prophets, Teachers, True Recorders[1]

The Survey by Questionnaire

Individual case studies such as those contained in the last section demonstrate the nature of some of the tensions that *can* exist between clergy and organists. However, they do not provide any information on the extent of the problem in the Church as a whole. It would have been quite impracticable for me to undertake a systematic visitation of hundreds of churches. Even if this had been possible, only in the most severe of cases would clergy/organist tensions be apparent to a visitor.

It therefore seemed clear to me that a survey by means of questionnaire was the only solution. In the light of the case studies, readers may already be mentally composing some suitable questions!

The Type of Survey

There are two sides to every disagreement. Clearly in order for the survey to be meaningful it was essential to obtain the views of organists as well as those of clergy. Since I would be asking clergy and organists to provide information on, amongst other things, their relationship with each other, I decided to provide a separate questionnaire for each, to be

---

[1] P. Dearmer, [in, for example,] *Songs of Praise Enlarged Edition* (OUP, London, 1931), No. 212.

returned in separate prepaid envelopes. In choosing the questions, I had to strike a compromise between seeking as much information as possible, and not making undue demands on respondents' time. In addition, certain questions could not reasonably be asked because of their sensitive nature. Such questions included: (to the musical director) 'How satisfied are you with your vicar's theological and liturgical competence?'; and (to both parties) 'Do you believe that your vicar/musical director is a practising Christian?'

The Church of England has, within the ranks of its faithful, widely differing opinions on almost every aspect of worship, and there are almost equally wide variations in its terminology. Some seemingly unambiguous words have different meanings in different contexts. Conversely, different branches of the Church use different words to mean the same thing. I tried to eliminate misunderstanding by specially defining in the questionnaires certain terms and, in order to assume a neutral stance, adopted certain composite terms.

My first task was to identify the person with overall pastoral responsibility for a church. He/she might be known locally as: Rector, Team Rector, Vicar, Team Vicar, Minister (evangelical), Minister-in-charge (evangelical and/or a lay person in charge of a daughter church), Priest-in-charge. The term 'Clergy-in-charge', although neutral in tone, would in some instances have been factually incorrect. I therefore adopted the slightly clumsy term *priest/minister-in-charge*. The strength of feeling on this matter can be gauged from the fact that one clergyman who completed the questionnaire deleted the word 'minister' every time that it appeared. On occasions in the rest of this book, the term will be abbreviated to 'priest-in-charge' or, where there is no question of ambiguity, simply 'priest'.

Strictly speaking, the person in charge of the music at a church is the priest/minister-in-charge. I therefore made a point in the questionnaires of defining the *musical director* as: 'the person who for practical purposes bears overall responsibility for music at a church'. Such a person has hitherto been the organist but, given their current shortage, and the increasing use of instrumental groups, this is no longer necessarily the case. On the one hand, there was the risk of frightening off some potential respondents who could not see themselves as having so grandiose a title. Conversely, the word 'organist' would discourage, for example, someone who had been accompanying all the services on a piano for the last five years because no organist could be found. A recent survey[1] in predominantly evangelical churches has found that the job title of the music leader was 'music(al) director' or 'director of music' in 25% of cases, 'music coordinator' in 5% and 'worship leader' in 4% of cases. Another survey reported the use of 'music(al) director', 'director of music' or 'music coordinator' in a third of the sample.[2] In addition, the term 'minister of music' is used increasingly in certain churches, especially in America, to emphasise the pastoral nature of the post.

I defined a *choir* as: 'a group of singers (robed or unrobed) remaining *together* during a service, even when they are not singing'. A group defined in this way would probably be expected to lead, at least nominally, the congregational singing.

If a church did not have its own *parochial church council* (for example because it was a daughter church), in those questions relating to the PCC, respondents were asked to answer in terms of their own church's nearest equivalent. In many evangelical churches, hymns are known as songs, so the composite term *hymns/congregational songs* was used.

Although I was fortunate enough to meet most of the clergy at chapter meetings, I needed some means of presenting the project to the others and to all the musical directors. They were being asked to give of their time, and to answer questions of a confidential and potentially compromising nature. I therefore sent a covering letter, explaining the

---

[1] 'Results of Your Completed Questionnaire Forms' in *Music in Worship*, 39 (Summer 1987), p. 6.

[2] *A Joyful Noise* (Resource Paper 84:7) (Administry, St. Albans, 1984), p. 5.

project, and reassuring them that it had diocesan backing, and that their confidentiality would be respected. I signed each letter and, in the case of the clergy one, wrote the priest's name at the head of the page. Respondents were invited to send a stamped addressed envelope for a summary of the results: one in eight did so.

A priest responsible for more than one church would receive an appropriate number of questionnaires. Since the questionnaires were going to be analysed on a church-by-church basis, he would need some means of knowing which questionnaire referred to which church. If the name of the church were written on the questionnaire itself, and it subsequently went astray in the post, then the information would cease to be confidential. I therefore wrote on the questionnaire a serial number, and on each priest's covering letter the serial number(s) and name of the respective church(es). Similarly, it was not beyond the bounds of possibility that a musical director might be responsible for more than one church and receive questionnaires either from the same or even from two different priests. To avoid confusion, I wrote the serial number and name of the church on each musical director's covering letter.

The Area of the Survey

Survey results based on a small sample cannot be regarded as reliable, and my original aim was to examine up to a thousand churches in different types of diocese. However, before embarking on this, I wanted to test the question-naires' effectiveness in a pilot study. This began in January 1988 in the hundred churches of four deaneries in the Diocese of Oxford. It was soon clear that the questionnaires of both parties were being completed as intended, and returned in quite large numbers. This very success, however, gave rise to a new problem. I had always intended to type the data into the computer personally (indeed I had no budget for a separate typist!), but had not anticipated the sheer magnitude of the task. Had the project continued on the scale originally envisaged, the task would have become totally impracticable. I decided therefore only to extend the pilot study to eight further deaneries in the Oxford Diocese. This brought the total for the project to 298 of the 826 churches, in twelve of the 29 deaneries in the diocese. The distribution of questionnaires in the remainder of the project took place between June 1988 and February 1989.

The Diocese of Oxford covers 2222 square miles, making it the fifth largest in the Church of England. Its northern tip is only 30 miles from Birmingham, in the East it is within 12 miles of Central London, while its south-western corner is within 25 miles of Salisbury. Its total population in mid-1987 was 1,948,000.

Apart from its size, Oxford may be regarded as a very 'average' diocese. Calculations on data taken from *Church Statistics*[1] yielded the following information for each of the 43 dioceses in the Church of England: population per square mile, population per church, percentage of population on church electoral rolls, and number of Sunday church attendances per 1000 population. Nineteen dioceses had a lower population per square mile than Oxford (whose value was 877), 22 had a higher. Fifteen dioceses had a lower population per church, 27 had a higher. Oxford's value was 2358. Its proportion of population on church electoral rolls was 3.4%, twenty dioceses had a higher figure, 22 a lower one. Finally, Oxford noted 28 Sunday church attendances per 1000 population: fifteen dioceses recorded a higher figure, 27 a lower one. We may therefore regard the Diocese of Oxford as typical in several important respects, and any conclusions drawn from the present survey may reasonably be taken to apply in other dioceses also.

Distribution and Return of Questionnaires

Even with diocesan approval, any questionnaire arriving 'cold' on a vicarage doormat might easily go straight into a

---

[1] *Church Statistics: Some facts and figures about the Church of England* (Central Board of Finance of the Church of England, London, 1989), pp. 1–39.

wastepaper-basket. This could be overcome, but not very efficiently, by my telephoning each priest-in-charge to seek his approval before sending the questionnaire to him. A method more effectively demonstrating official support was for me to distribute the questionnaires personally at a chapter meeting, address the meeting, and invite questions. This proved possible in ten of the twelve deaneries, and seemed to work very successfully. In some cases, I was invited to the lunch which accompanied the meeting. On these occasions I normally provided some sherry — I am uncertain whether this had any effect on the response rate. In the remaining two deaneries, there was either no chapter meeting scheduled for the immediate future, or its agenda was already full. In these cases, I telephoned each priest-in-charge before posting the questionnaires.

There appeared to be no equivalent way of making contact with the musical directors. For those churches affiliated to the Royal School of Church Music, there is an identifiable RSCM correspondent, but frequently he/she is not the musical director. In any case, less than half the churches were affiliated. The name and telephone number of the musical director could in principle be obtained from the priest or a churchwarden (whose name and address could be found in the *Diocesan Year Book*[1]). However, I felt that musical directors would be at least as likely as the clergy to take an interest in such a survey, and might well need less persuasion to complete their questionnaires. I therefore decided to ask the clergy to pass on the musical directors' questionnaires. The risk of a priest either deliberately or accidentally failing to do so seemed to be fairly heavily outweighed by the savings in both time and postage.[2]

In most cases, the questionnaires were returned within six weeks of their distribution. However, if after two months the

---

[1]   *Oxford Diocesan Year Book 1988* (Oxford Diocesan Board of Finance, Oxford, 1987).

[2]   The envelope containing the musical director's questionnaire and covering letter was unsealed, so that the priest might be reassured to know at least the questions being asked, even if he would not learn the responses to them.

priest's questionnaire had not been returned, he was given a reminder. This took the form of a telephone call, preferably to him personally, or, failing that, to a member of his family or his answering machine. Failure to respond was generally caused by pressure of other work rather than hostility to the questionnaire although, even in the latter case, many clergy were amenable to persuasion. By this stage, however, some of the questionnaires had already been consigned to the wastepaper-basket. In some cases, the questionnaires had been put safely aside to be completed in a spare moment — and lost. In either of the last two situations, if the priest expressed willingness to complete a duplicate questionnaire, he generally did so. If neither party's questionnaire had been returned, again the priest was approached in the first instance. If only the musical director's questionnaire was missing, he/she was reminded by telephone. If necessary, a second reminder was sent after a further two months.

In a very few cases, questionnaires were returned unanswered, usually with a covering letter. Some of the reasons given are listed below.

- 'Questionnaire has no relevance whatever to St X church.' (The person concerned was subsequently telephoned and was persuaded to dictate his responses to the questionnaire over the telephone.)
- 'Questionnaire much too long and complicated to be attempted.' (The letter explaining this was itself very long, and yielded a fair amount of useful information.)
- 'I am afraid that I do not have the time to give the questionnaire the attention that it deserves.'
- 'I never complete questionnaires unless I am forced to.'

The Analysis

The data analysis was performed by SAS (Statistical Analysis System) on VAX computers at Oxford University Computing Service.

The Response Rate

The response rate of the musical directors was 71%, slightly lower than the clergy 78%. However, since the questionnaires were distributed to the directors via their respective priest, it is likely that at least some never reached them at all, so making their true response rate at least comparable to that of the clergy.

OUTCOME OF DISTRIBUTION OF QUESTIONNAIRES

MUSICAL DIRECTOR		PRIEST-IN-CHARGE	
Total distributed	298	Total distributed	298
Completed by MD	175	Completed	231
Completed by PC		Interregnum[1]	6
acting as MD	11 [2]		
Churches without MD	14		
Churches without music	11		
Not completed	87	Not completed	61
Response rate	71%	Response rate[3]	78%

In the recent ACCMUS survey, 680 forms were distributed to clergy and 545 were returned, a response rate of 80%. It would appear from the Report[4] that the 680 were selected on the basis that they had all replied to an earlier survey on

[1] In some cases, parts of the questionnaire were completed either by another member of the clergy or a churchwarden.

[2] In the absence of any sort of musical leader, certain clergy saw themselves in the role by default. Others simply recorded the absence of a musical director. Even in the latter case, parts of the questionnaire were often completed. The distinction between the two cases is, however, somewhat arbitrary and may represent nothing more than the amount of time that the priest had available when attending to the questionnaires. In all subsequent analysis, where the views of musical directors are being compared with those of the clergy, such duplicated results will be excluded from the directors' set. In other cases, churchwardens saw themselves in the role by default.

[3] In two deaneries, the questionnaires were distributed to clergy by post rather than personally at a chapter meeting. This did not seem to affect the response rate.

[4] Jacqui Cooper, *Music in Parish Worship* (Central Board of Finance of the Church of England, London, [dated] 1990 [but not published until 1992]).

church finance — an ingenious way of maximising the response rate to the ACCMUS survey. There are, however, dangers in such an approach in that the sample of 680 may then not be sufficiently representative of the Church of England as a whole. A paper on clergy response rates to questionnaires has recently been published.[1]

[1] Robin L.D. Rees and Leslie J. Francis, 'Clergy response Rates to Work-Related Questionnaires: A Relationship Between Age, Work Load, and Burnout?' in *Social Behavior and Personality* 19, No. 1 (1991), pp. 45–51.

3

Captains Of The Saintly Band[1]

Musical Directors and Priests:
Their Similarities and Differences

Given the recent upheavals and the reported cases of conflict between clergy and church musicians, I wanted to investigate the situation at churches, as seen through the eyes of the musical director on the one hand, and the priest-in-charge on the other. However, I also wanted to analyse the characteristics of the respondents themselves, to see whether their differences of background or of general attitude could be related to the differences in their perception of the situation at their particular church.

In this chapter therefore, we focus our attention on two different species — *musical directors* on the one hand and *priests/ministers-in-charge* on the other. We note similarities and differences in their personal characteristics: sex, age and education, before moving on to compare their general attitudes to worship and to church music.[2]

---

[1] J.B. de Santeuil, tr. H.W. Baker, [in, for example,] *Hymns Ancient and Modern Revised* (Clowes, Beccles, 1950), No. 507.

[2] Many clergy and some musical directors were responsible for more than one church and, as such, completed more than one questionnaire. The numbers of musical directors and priests who completed questionnaires (as opposed to the number of questionnaires that they completed) were 165 and 125 respectively, and the results of this chapter are based on these figures. In other words, a priest in charge of, for example, four churches is counted only once.

General Characteristics

When I looked at musical directors, I found that the ratio of
men to women was just over two to one. This compares
with four to one a few years earlier,[1] so the organ console
is now far from being an all-male preserve. Although the
same cannot at present be said for the vicar's stall — the
ratio of males to females for ministers-in-charge was over a
hundred to one — it will be interesting to see if there is any
significant change in this figure by the turn of the century.
In the clergy questionnaire, the question concerning sex was
postponed until page 4: a clergyman hostile to the ordination
of women might have become equally hostile to the questionnaire if he had been asked his sex as the very first
question. Indeed, one respondent deleted the word 'sex'
altogether and substituted 'gender'.

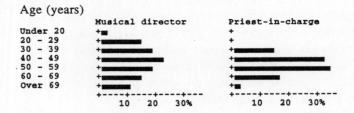

The most common age range of musical directors was
40–49, that of clergy 50–59, their estimated[2] average ages
being 47.6 and 50.6 respectively. The youngest musical
director was only fourteen years old and, sadly perhaps, was

[1] Berkeley Hill, *A Survey of Church Music, 1982* (Royal School of Church
    Music, Addington, 1983), p. 38.
[2] One may reasonably assume that the average age of those within a given age
    group is midway between the limits. In other words, a reasonable estimate of
    the average age of the group aged between 20 and 29 is 24.5. In this way one
    can obtain an estimate of the average age of the full set of respondents. The
    average age of those 'under 20' and 'over 69' is a little more difficult to
    ascertain, but common sense would suggest values of about 18 and 72
    respectively. Moreover, since there are likely to be relatively few in either
    category, even quite a large change in either of these figures would have very
    little influence on the value of the estimated average of the full set.

prevented by his mother from answering some of the more contentious questions.

Several other matters of a general nature emerged from the early questions. A high proportion of the clergy had entered the ministry early in life, and almost two thirds had been in the ministry for 20 years or more. These points are illustrated in the charts below. One in forty was in either post-retirement or non-stipendiary ministry, the rest in stipendiary. Only one in fifty had studied part-time for ordination. The main profession of almost a third of the musical directors was (or had been) in the field of music.

Priest-in-charge's time in secular employment
before ministerial training

Period since completion of priest-in-charge's training

Musical Ability

Next I wanted to discover the levels of musical attainment of our two parties. I therefore asked: 'If you have ever attended instrumental or singing lessons, what was your approximate level of attainment?'

Attainment level

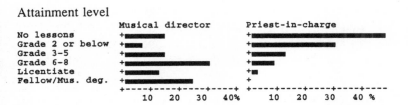

A third of the musical directors had Grade 5 or less, but an equal number held a Licentiate or above. In 1982, the proportion in the latter group was found to be as high as a half.[1] (This discrepancy may well be caused by a major turnover of directors since 1982 — we look at evidence for this on page 127 — or perhaps those responding to the earlier survey, all at RSCM-affiliated churches, were unrepresentative in their high level of musical activity.) Half the clergy had never received any tuition at all, while a further third had reached only Grade 2 or lower. In the circumstances, I find the ACCMUS statement: 'Most clergy have at least some musical knowledge'[2] quite surprising, and wonder on what data it is based. The average for musical directors fell at about Grades 6-8.

Musical Training in Theological Colleges

Having noted the clergy's lack of musical expertise, we may reasonably ask whether they were given adequate opportunity for studying the use of music in worship during their ministerial training. I began by asking how many hours had been devoted to this.

Time spent on musical study during ministerial training

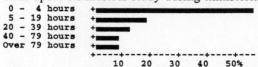

During the course of their entire ministerial training, a majority of the clergy had spent four hours or less studying the use of music in worship. Three quarters had spent less than twenty hours. The average was eighteen. (A few clergy indicated that they had included the time of college choir practice, and others may well have done so without recording the fact. The time actually spent on study would there-

---

[1] Berkeley Hill, *A Survey of Church Music, 1982* (Royal School of Church Music, Addington, 1983), p. 32.

[2] *In Tune With Heaven*, Report of the Archbishops' Commission on Church Music (Church House Publishing, and Hodder and Stoughton, London, 1992), p. 191.

fore be even lower than these figures suggest.) Did they feel
that this was adequate in quantity and quality?

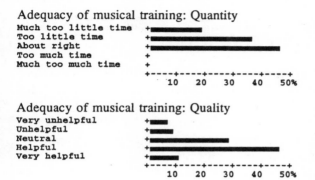

Adequacy of musical training: Quantity

Over half the clergy felt that the time had been either too
little or much too little. Although it is likely that some of
the participants in the survey were not in the least interested
in music, not a single one felt the training to have been
excessive. Almost half felt that they had derived no benefit
from their musical training, whilst almost two thirds were
not satisfied with its quantity and/or quality. Combining
these figures with data elsewhere in the questionnaire, I also
discovered that the catholic colleges have always spent more
time in music-training than their evangelical and middle-of-
the road counterparts. Worryingly, during the last thirty
years the time spent in musical training has actually fallen
at all types of college!

Musical Refresher Courses

Given the above, it was important to discover how widely
musical directors and clergy were availing themselves of the
church-music refresher courses run by the RSCM and other
bodies, and whether these courses were felt to be helpful.
Three quarters of the clergy had not attended such a course
since ministerial training, and an equal proportion of musical
directors had not done so in the last three years. However,
those attending had usually found them helpful or very
helpful.

Helpfulness of courses

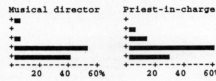

In a survey undertaken by the Music in Worship Trust, nearly three fifths of the church musicians were attending regional training courses.[1] Even allowing for the fact that the report fails to define 'musicians' (the director or the whole choir?), and the nature and frequency of the courses, this figure seems commendably high.

Had our respondents, either as children or as adults, ever sung in a church choir? In other words, had they at some time in their lives been receiving regular training, however minimal, in church music? Two fifths of the clergy and a quarter of the musical directors had never done so. The latter figure may seem surprisingly high, but half of these directors were women, to whom the traditional all-male choir would have been be a closed door.

Levels of Education

Having looked at specifically musical qualifications, we now take a look at the priests' and musical directors' qualifications in general. Both groups of respondents were asked whether they held the following: fellowship and/or first degree in music, first degree in theology, first degree in any other subject, higher degree in any subject, church music qualification with liturgical content (e.g. Archbishop's Diploma or Certificate, rather than ARCO(CHM)), teacher-training certificate, and other professional qualifications.

---

[1] 'Results of Your Completed Questionnaire Forms' in *Music in Worship*, 39 (Summer 1987), p. 5.

Qualification

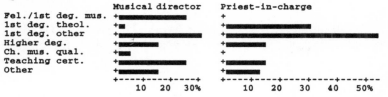

Roughly a third of the clergy held a degree in theology, slightly higher than the proportion of musical directors holding a comparable qualification in music. (The musical directors holding degrees in theology all turned out to be assistant priests holding also high musical qualifications. However, a further one in six of the directors had undertaken some form of adult theological or pastoral training course — in at least one case to the level of Lay Reader.)

A qualification in church music should in theory be a point of contact between musicians and the clergy, but the results from this question are not encouraging. Most clergy lacked the necessary practical skills to take such an examination (Grade 5 Practical was until recently demanded as a prerequisite for the ACertCM), whilst the musicians seemed to lack the interest. We will be looking at this point again on page 98. Qualifications in the 'other' category were for the musical directors in social work, management, librarianship, physics, and theology. For the clergy they were in accountancy, administration, engineering, the Law Society and the Civil Service.

In order to obtain a still broader view, I counted the number of qualifications of each respondent. Ordination was included as a qualification, as was a licentiate in music.

Number of qualifications

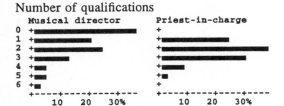

On these admittedly arbitrary criteria, the clergy appeared to be significantly more highly qualified, although less obviously so amongst the real high-flyers. The average number of qualifications for musical directors was 1.4, for clergy 2.3.

Membership of Church Musical Associations

By this stage it had become apparent that there was no real point of contact between clergy and musical directors as far as academic study was concerned. Was there perhaps anything more hopeful when it came to membership of church-related musical associations? Since membership implies a potential receptiveness to new ideas, I asked both parties whether they belonged to: the Royal School of Church Music (as a *personal member*), Guild of Church Musicians, local branch of the Incorporated Association of Organists, Royal College of Organists, Friends of Cathedral Music, Music in Worship Trust, and any other associations.

Membership of musical associations

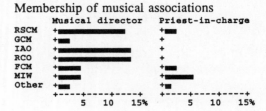

Of all the church music associations, the one most directly influential is the RSCM. We will be looking at church-membership of the RSCM on pages 98 and 121), but personal membership implies a somewhat deeper interest on the part of the individual. Few, however, held such membership. The Incorporated Association of Organists is an educational charity, taking its present title in 1929.[1] It works at local level with almost 100 regional centres, nationally and internationally, to advance the knowledge and

[1] Roger Bishton, 'The Incorporated Association of Organists' in *Church Music Quarterly*, October 1985, pp. 8–9.

enjoyment of the organ and its music. Whilst not involved expressly with *church* music, the IAO does nevertheless provide a forum for organists to exchange ideas with each other but not, it would appear, with the clergy. However, less than one in seven even of the musical directors seem to avail themselves of the opportunity.

Since 1957 the Friends of Cathedral Music have been fostering the welfare of cathedral music through regional gatherings of its members, grants to assist choral foundations, etc. Their free booklet *Singing in Cathedrals*, published annually in conjunction with several other bodies, lists the times of all choral services at cathedrals and collegiate chapels. (We have already noted on page 20 the recent FCM survey of the most widely-sung cathedral music.) Cathedral music is very far removed from that found nowadays in most parish churches, and this perhaps explains why its membership was so low among those taking part in the survey. Lower still was the level of membership of the Guild of Church Musicians. The Music in Worship Trust (now called Music and Worship Foundation) is predominantly evangelical in outlook but, even in this wing of the Church, membership among musical directors was very low. However, clergy membership was higher here than for other organisations. Other musical associations had even less support. Two of those specified were purely local groups, the third was the Christian Music Association, mentioned on page 59.

In isolation the above figures give no clue as to whether the membership was evenly spread, or whether a few people belonged to many organisations. The table below, showing the number of organisations to which each respondent belonged, remedies this: the more organisations, in all probability the greater the commitment.

Number of organisations *excluding* church affiliation

```
      Musical director        Priest-in-charge
0     +█████████████████      +████████████████████
1     +████████               +██
2     +█                      +
3     +█                      +
      +---+---+---+---+--      +---+---+---+---+--
        20  40  60  80%          20  40  60  80%
```

Some two thirds of the musical directors and nine out of ten clergy held no personal membership. *Church affiliation* to the RSCM (as opposed to personal membership) is another potential measure of commitment and interest. It is, however, less direct in that the church treasurer may be paying the RSCM subscription each year, without either the priest or the musical director necessarily availing themselves of the benefits of membership. Notwithstanding this, if affiliation *or* personal RSCM membership scores 1 point (but instances of membership *and* affiliation count only once), the charts then take the following form.

Number of organisations *including* church affiliation

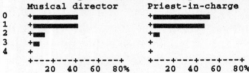

More than two fifths of the musical directors and more than half the clergy did not have access to the news and views of any of the church-related musical associations. This surely is not a healthy situation. (We will be looking further into church affiliation to the RSCM on page 121.) Despite this, I wondered whether respondents might be interested in joining with other clergy and musicians in a discussion group on music and worship.

Level of interest in a discussion group

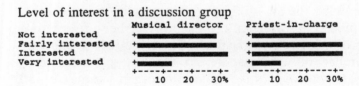

The level of interest of both parties was only moderate for a meeting which might help resolve or even avoid misunderstanding between them, thereby perhaps enriching a church's worship. There was possibly the feeling that discussing matters in general terms would not be particularly productive. A few clergy and directors expressed interest, but felt that they could not spare the time.

Differing Ideas for Worship

Do musical directors and clergy, as two separate groups, have significantly differing ideas for what constitutes worship? Three common measures for this are charismatic/non-charismatic, catholic/evangelical, and liberal/conservative. Of these, the last seemed to have the least influence on church music, so I did not pursue it. Instead I asked both parties to indicate their preferences concerning the other two. This provoked a number of comments, some hostile. From the directors these included: *don't understand*; or more extremely *don't understand and don't want to*; *don't understand in the context of music* (it was not intended to be taken in this context!); *does not apply* (probably a variation of the previous response); *I am not prepared to answer*; *I want traditional* (a frequent response); or even *Agnostic (traditional)*. From the clergy there were fewer comments. One indicated that he had attempted to answer the questions in a musical sense (e.g. evangelical choruses vs. gregorian chants). Others expressed dissatisfaction at being asked to categorise worship in this way.

The question on charismatic worship produced a significantly lower response rate than other questions, especially amongst the musical directors. This may well be because, unless they were involved in the Charismatic Movement, many would not understand the meaning of the word. The comments mentioned above provide some evidence of this. However, several of the clergy felt that the word was too imprecise. In addition to its colloquial sense of freedom of expression in worship, even possibly speaking in tongues as at Pentecost ('glossalia'), it could also simply mean worship guided by the Holy Spirit.

Charismatic worship: personal preferences

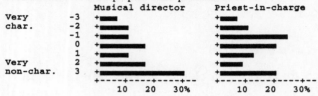

The form of the charts is strange. In the case of the musical directors, with the exception of a minor peak in the middle, there is a clear majority preferring to avoid charismatic worship. For the clergy, there is a peak of those preferring mildly charismatic worship and a second, smaller, peak of those preferring to avoid it. The averages of the two groups are respectively 0.8 and 0.3.

Catholic/evangelical worship: personal preferences

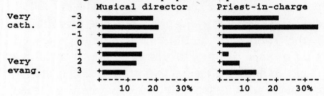

Most musical directors seemed to favour worship towards the catholic end of the spectrum, although there was a secondary peak in the mildly evangelical area. This, strangely, is a viewpoint which found least favour amongst the clergy, whose chart has a main peak at the fairly strong catholic stance, and a smaller one at the strongly evangelical. The average figure for musical directors is -0.5, for clergy -0.9.

The Ideal Musical Director

What qualities should we be looking for in the ideal musical director? Are these absolute, or are certain qualities important simply because the individual priest perceives them to be important?

In an attempt to obtain an insight into this, I asked both parties to indicate their views on each of the following criteria for appointing a musical director to a church:

- Church music qualification with liturgical content (e.g. Archbishop's Diploma or Certificate);
- Other qualifications in music;
- School-teaching qualification;
- Ability to play hymns and other congregational music well;
- Ability as a solo organist;
- Liturgical awareness;
- Musical director is a practising Christian;
- Pastoral gifts;
- Administrative ability;
- Willingness to co-operate in a flexible way;
- Involvement with other church-based activities;
- Involvement with 'non-traditional' church music;
- Ability in training young (under-16) choir members;
- Ability in training adult members;
- Ability to attract and retain a choir.

I asked them to give their responses on a scale from 1 (very advantageous), through 2 (advantageous), 3 (not relevant) and 4 (disadvantageous) to 5 (very disadvantageous). The table overleaf shows the average values, as perceived by the musical director and priest respectively.

Criteria for Appointing a Musical Director

Musical director's view		Priest-in-charge's view

VERY ADVANTAGEOUS — 1.0

— 1.1

— 1.2

Hymn-playing ability —— 1.3 —— Hymn-playing ability
Willingness to cooperate
Practising Christian; Attract/
retain choir
— 1.4 —— Liturgical awareness

Attract/retain choir —— 1.5
Willingness to co-operate —— —— Adult choir training
Practising Christian —— 1.6 —— Children's choir training
Young choir training ——
Adult choir training == 1.7

Liturgical awareness —— 1.8 —— 'Ordinary music' qual.

'Ordinary music' qual. —— 1.9 Church-music qual.
Non-traditional music
Solo organist
ADVANTAGEOUS — 2.0 —— Pastoral gifts
Solo organist == —— Admin. ability
Admin. ability 2.1 —— Other church activities

Church-music qual. —— 2.2
Pastoral gifts == —— School-teaching qual.
Other church activities 2.3

Non-traditional music —— 2.4

— 2.5

School-teaching qual. —— 2.6

NOT RELEVANT ↓ 3.0 ↓

DISADVANTAGEOUS ↓ 4.0 ↓

VERY DISADVANTAGEOUS ↓ 5.0 ↓

We see from the table that neither party held qualifications in church music in very high esteem. (In particular, one interpretation of the response of the two priests who found the qualification to be disadvantageous is that they might feel threatened by such a director.) This must be disappointing to the Archbishops, who have expressed the wish that: 'all who have the responsibility of leading the music of their church should aim to achieve [the ACertCM] as a basic, minimum acceptable standard'.[1] One crumb of comfort was that those musical directors who had taken such a qualification felt marginally more enthusiastic about it than those who had not. Both clergy and musical directors felt that qualifications in 'ordinary music' were more useful than qualifications in church music. Once more, musical directors were a little less impressed with such qualifications than were the clergy — who may in some cases have been only too well aware of the need for their musical director to be better qualified! Playing music for congregational singing was considered to be the most important factor of all those listed. Three quarters of both parties felt this to be 'very advantageous'. A possible view of those few clergy and directors who did not feel that the criterion was relevant may have been that the organ playing should be in the hands of an assistant. One musical director, after replying 'not relevant' for ability as a solo organist, remarked: 'You cannot do much on a harmonium'.

Clergy and musical directors were in marked disagreement over the benefits of 'liturgical awareness' (the musical director's detailed understanding of what is happening during the service so that, for example, a short interlude can be played, or indeed drawn to a conclusion, at the right moment). The religious conviction of the musical director was regarded as very important, both by the directors themselves and by the clergy. It may seem surprising that the clergy did not take a stronger line on the question of the musical director's religious conviction. However, one priest

---

[1] Prospectus of the Guild of Church Musicians (London, 1990), [p.3].

wrote on the questionnaire: 'You put up with whoever you can get', and this view may be reflected in the clergy's response to this criterion. Conversely, another priest commented:'very very advantageous', whilst no fewer than three musical directors felt it to be 'essential'. Despite the care I had taken in the questionnaires to avoid offence, one musical director found the term 'practising Christian' offensive, and felt that no-one should dare to claim to be one. Pastoral gifts, which might be defined as the ability to offer spiritual as well as musical leadership, were regarded more highly by the clergy than by the directors themselves, one of whom wrote: 'don't understand' against this criterion. Administrative ability includes advance planning (such as ordering music in time for a special service), and ability to communicate orally and in writing with others. Surprisingly perhaps, neither party rated this particularly highly.

Much more important was whether a musical director was willing to co-operate in a flexible way, by implication with the priest. The readiness of the priest to co-operate with the musical director would probably be another interesting field of study. One musical director, having indicated that he viewed the criterion with favour, added the cri de coeur: 'but not with too-trendy guitar-charged clergy'.

The use of modern or popular music in worship was a particularly controversial issue within, as well as between, the parties. The clergy were not quite so strongly in favour as I had expected, while the musical directors took an even more cautious view. In the words of one: 'From with-it parsons etc., Good Lord deliver us'. The ability to attract and retain a choir implies actively developing the music, rather than merely accepting the status quo. Even in these days, with much emphasis on congregational music, this criterion was regarded by both parties as very important. Indeed it was considered to be more important than actually being able to train the choir effectively. A possible reason for this, at least among the clergy, is that a choir is seen as a way of encouraging both children and adults to become more actively involved in the life of the church, and even to draw in young and old from outside. Several directors and clergy at churches without choirs regarded the criterion as irrelevant, possibly because they had given up all hope of ever having a choir.

In summary, the musical directors seemed to place more emphasis on the purely musical aspects of their work than did the clergy, resulting in a wider range of figures (from 1.25 to 2.56, compared with 1.28 to 2.24). To put it another way, the directors were looking for specialist musicians, the clergy for all-rounders. However, there appeared to be further similarities between the figures of the two groups. They selected the same seven most important criteria (hymn playing, attract/retain choir, willingness to co-operate, practising Christian, children's choir training, adult choir training, liturgical awareness), even though they did not agree on the order of the seven. In both cases there was then a gap, followed by 'ordinary music' qualification. There was then a further gap followed by the seven remaining, less advantageous, criteria. Again the parties did not agree on the ordering of these.

The Ideal Church

So much for the ideal musical director — what about the ideal church? I asked the directors to give me their views on the following:
• Church near to home;
• Large congregation;
• High salary;
• Good choir;
• Good organ;
• Musically qualified priest-in-charge;
• Priest-in-charge and director sharing a common approach to music;
• Priest-in-charge and director sharing a common approach to worship.
As before, the scale was from 1 (very advantageous), through 2 (advantageous), 3 (not relevant) and 4 (disadvan-

tageous) to 5 (very disadvantageous). The average values are shown overleaf.

The directors felt it important to see eye to eye with the clergy over music. Agreement over worship was seen as marginally less important, perhaps partly because the two parties were less likely to be drawn into direct conflict. The relative positions of 'good organ' and 'good choir' suggest that directors saw themselves primarily as organists. However, this view was almost certainly coloured by the fact that many may never have had a choir to direct.

A church near to home saves both time and money, and a director may want to get involved in the local community. It would probably also help in the recruitment of a choir. A quarter of the musical directors were aged 60 or over, and a significant proportion of these might well not have a car. For such people, the dearth of public transport on a Sunday makes a local church even more desirable. However, there was no statistical evidence of the over-sixties ranking this criterion higher than their younger counterparts. Directors gave little attention to the salary (and there was no evidence of it assuming greater importance after retirement). Equally irrelevant seemed to be the question of whether the church was 'successful' in terms of congregation size. The most controversial matter was the question of the desirability of the priest holding a music qualification, no fewer than one director in six viewing the prospect with misgivings.

The directors' range of figures for these criteria in selecting a church was 1.70 to 2.90. However in the previous question, their range for a church selecting a musical director was markedly different (perceived as more important?) at 1.25 to 2.56.

Finally, one director added a further criterion, which was marked as 'very advantageous' — that the priest should be able to sing well and in tune. It would be interesting to know whether the absence of such an ability is regarded as a widespread problem.

Musical Directors' Criteria for Selecting a Church

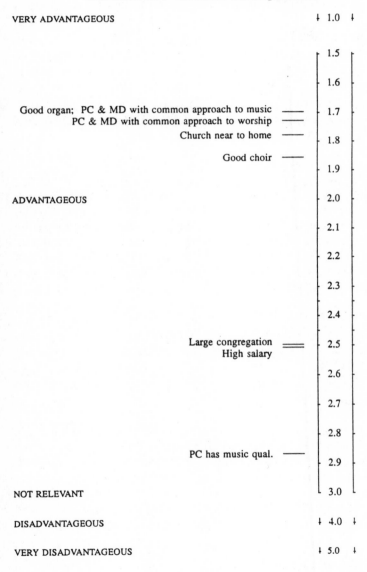

VERY ADVANTAGEOUS ǀ 1.0 ǀ

1.5

1.6

Good organ; PC & MD with common approach to music —— 1.7
PC & MD with common approach to worship ——
Church near to home —— 1.8

Good choir ——

1.9

ADVANTAGEOUS 2.0

2.1

2.2

2.3

2.4

Large congregation ═══ 2.5
High salary

2.6

2.7

2.8

PC has music qual. ——
2.9

NOT RELEVANT 3.0

DISADVANTAGEOUS ǀ 4.0 ǀ

VERY DISADVANTAGEOUS ǀ 5.0 ǀ

Hiring and Firing

Questions relating to 'industrial relations' between priest and musical director were very topical at the time of the survey. The hiring and, more controversially, the firing of organists or choirmasters had previously been solely in the hands of the priest-in-charge. However in 1988, after many years' discussion by a working party of the RSCM, and subsequently by General Synod, an amendment to Canon B20 (*Of the Hymns, Anthems and Music of the Church*) was finally ratified by Parliament. It now read:

> In all [parish] churches and chapels . . . the functions of appointing any organist or choirmaster (by whatever name called), and of terminating the appointment . . . shall be exercisable by the minister with the agreement of the parochial church council, except that if the archdeacon of the archdeaconry in which the parish is situated, in the case of termination of an appointment, considers that the circumstances are such that the agreement of the parochial church council should be dispensed with, the archdeacon may direct accordingly.[1]

The working party had originally requested that the appointment and its termination be in the hands of the PCC with the agreement of the priest, but this was found to be unacceptable to General Synod because the powers of the clergy were being undermined. However, in the words of the chairman of the working party:

> On reflection we felt that [the measure as adopted] would bring about what we were so anxious to achieve, namely the involvement of other persons in addition to the Incumbent as a safeguard against summary dismissal on inadequate grounds.[2]

I therefore asked the clergy whether they felt that the appointment of a musical director should remain the sole

---

[1] Quoted by Vincent Waterhouse, 'Organists' contracts: law change brings in PCCs' in *Church Music Quarterly*, October 1988, p. 8.

[2] Dame Betty Ridley, 'The security of parish church organists' in *Church Music Quarterly*, October 1985, p. 20.

ultimate responsibility of the priest-in-charge. Half voted 'yes', slightly under half 'no', and one in twenty undecided. Of those voting 'yes', some indicated that this was for ultimate rather than sole ultimate responsibility. Another commented: 'impossible to answer without knowing the priest, but I know that *I* would want the last word!'. Taking advice is somewhat different from taking decisions, so I asked: 'From which of the following would you seek advice before appointing a new musical director?'[1]

Parties consulted by priest when appointing a new musical director

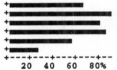

```
Other clergy                              +████████████████
Churchwardens                             +███████████████████
PCC                                       +██████████████████
The choir (assuming there were one)       +████████████████
Independent adviser (e.g. RSCM commissioner) +██████████
Others                                    +███
                                          +---+---+---+---+--
                                           20  40  60  80%
```

Two thirds of clergy would consult their colleagues before making an appointment. (I gave as much scope as possible for a positive answer, by not specifying whether 'other clergy' meant the priest's assistant, his peers in other parishes, or the rural dean.) The PCC would be consulted in roughly four fifths of cases, although Canon B20 now requires the PCC's agreement in all cases. A quarter of the clergy would consult other parties: these included the Incorporated Association of Organists, other local organists, the priest's wife, referees (although I trust that *no* organist would be appointed without references being taken up!), the entire church membership, and the heads of music at local schools. Almost four priests in five would seek advice from three or more parties. However, as one clergyman wryly remarked: 'There is seldom a choice'.

So what about the firing? I asked the clergy: 'In the event of dispute with the priest-in-charge, to which if any of the following do you think that a musical director should have the right of appeal?'

---

[1] In each case the chart shows the 'yes' responses as a percentage after 'don't know' responses have been excluded.

Parties to whom priests would allow their musical directors
the right of appeal

Other clergy
Churchwardens
The PCC
Independent adviser (e.g. RSCM commissioner)
Others

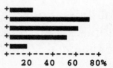

20   40   60   80%

This seemed rather less popular. Only one priest in five
would wish to involve fellow-clergy in a dispute, despite the
fact that, once again, I gave as much scope as possible for
a positive answer. This perhaps suggests a feeling of
insecurity. Just over two thirds of the clergy would be
willing for the churchwardens to be approached, but to what
extent they would be allowed to overturn a clergy decision
is unclear. Indeed one clergyman wrote: 'Would the appeal
seek to resolve differences, or override the vicar's authority?
If the latter, it would be an impossible situation.' The PCC
was felt to be rather less suitable for this task than the
wardens, possibly for reasons of maintaining confidentiality.
However, in accordance with Canon B20, it would now have
to be involved if the dispute led to a dismissal. Less popular
was the prospect of bringing in an outsider, another possible
sign of clergy insecurity. Of those clergy agreeing to an
appeal elsewhere, some specified that it should be to
deanery or diocesan level presumably, but not necessarily,
to be heard by a senior member of the clergy. Others
suggested a mutually acceptable conciliator.

As before, I counted the *number* of different parties to
whom appeal would be allowed. Just over half of the clergy
would allow appeal to two or more parties, while a further
third would allow appeal to one party. However, it is
perhaps alarming that as many as one in ten of the clergy
would not seem to allow appeal to anyone at all. Indeed in
virtually all such cases, the response consistently took the
form of 'no' rather than merely a 'don't know'.

It would have been fascinating to discover the extent to
which disputes had actually arisen, and the success or
otherwise of any appeals.

Summary

The priests/ministers-in-charge are almost exclusively male, the musical directors predominantly so and marginally younger. There is a wide range of musical ability amongst musical directors, whilst that of the clergy is heavily concentrated at the lower end. Similarly, directors' knowledge of theology is extremely limited. Here we see a fundamental difference in the outlook of our two parties, with very little common ground between them. Clergy seem to be more highly qualified academically than musical directors. Very few directors and none of the clergy have taken any formal qualification in church music, nor does either party see much value in such a qualification. However, clergy are unhappy with their theological-college training on the use of music in worship.

There is little interest, especially among the clergy, in membership of church-related musical associations. Few of either group have attended courses (formal or informal) in church music, nor does there appear to be any great enthusiasm for joining a discussion group on the subject. However, those that have attended courses have found them helpful.

The two parties have different views on what is expected of directors, especially in the importance of directors' liturgical awareness, and involvement in non-traditional music.

Postscript

Somewhat mischievously, I asked the clergy how they felt about the level of funds provided by the Church of England for lay training in music. Half did not know, a third felt it was inadequate, a sixth felt it was about right, while one person felt it was too high. Only one respondent seemed to spot the deliberate catch in the question. He commented: 'I was unaware that the C. of E. provided any!'.

4

O Faith Of England[1]

The Church and its People

There is a saying that the greatest resource of any organisation is its personnel. Even from a secular standpoint, this is no less true of the Church, while most Christians would argue that God is scarcely likely to act other than through some human agency.

In this chapter we look at church personnel, the groups that they form and, as a particular example of this, the choir.[2]

Preliminaries

I included some initial questions of a more general nature, as their data enabled me to test whether my sample was representative of the Church of England as a whole. I wondered also whether the state of a particular aspect of a church's life might prove to be a pointer to the state of that church's music. In addition, I (or indeed someone else) might in due course wish to re-examine the survey data from a completely different viewpoint, in which case this information might well come in useful.

---

[1] T.A. Lacey, [in, for example,] *The English Hymnal* (New Edition) (OUP and Mowbray, London, 1933), No. 544.
[2] We will be looking at the musical director in Chapter 5.

First then, in what types of area were the churches situated?

Area served by the church

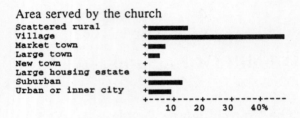

Churches in a village comprised the largest single category, just under half the total. The last five categories may be termed non-rural, and comprised a third.[1] Closely associated with type of area will be the population in a church's catchment area.

Population in church's catchment area

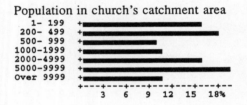

This varied enormously: the smallest was 27, the greatest 25,000, nonetheless one church in ten was responsible for 10,000 souls, an extremely heavy pastoral burden. The average was 3402. While these estimates by the clergy are less likely to be accurate than official statistics — averages in 1987 for the Oxford Diocese[2] and for the Church of

---

[1] The precise figure was 32.1%. This is in reasonable agreement with the corresponding figure of 30.5% calculated from information provided by Francis, and taken from a survey of more than 7000 churches (Leslie J. Francis and David W. Lankshear, *Continuing in the Way* (National Society (Church of England) for Promoting Religious Education, London, 1991)). It provides evidence of the representative nature of the present sample.

[2] *Oxford Diocesan Year Book, 1988* (Oxford Diocesan Board of Finance, Oxford, 1987).

England[1] were 2358 and 2897 respectively — the level of agreement still suggests a reasonably representative sample.

Next I asked the Church of England's standard questions on congregation size, namely the numbers of Easter and Christmas communicants, and electoral roll figures. However, communicant figures under-estimate attendance by ignoring non-communicants and those attending non-eucharistic services; conversely festival figures tend to be abnormally high because of the number of casual attenders. Furthermore, electoral roll figures will depend on how rigorously the priest allows only active church members to join.[2]

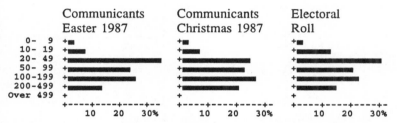

In general, the charts do not make encouraging reading. Two fifths of the churches had fewer than 50 Easter communicants, and one church in thirteen had less than twenty. The range was enormous: from less than ten to over 500, with an average of 96. At Christmas the average was 120, but again with one church in thirteen reporting fewer than twenty communicants. Larger churches seemed to do better at Christmas than at Easter. The largest figure reported was 700. We will be looking at sizes of congregation at normal services on page 146. Another somewhat disturbing statistic is the fact that one church in eight reported fewer than twenty people on its electoral roll. Since those on the roll are probably bearing most of the costs, not least repair of the fabric, there must be some doubt as to how long the present situation can continue at these churches. The average

---

[1] *Church Statistics: Some facts and figures about the Church of England* (Central Board of Finance of the Church of England, London, 1989).
[2] Leslie J. Francis, *Rural Anglicanism* (Collins, London, 1985), p. 22.

was 96. The averages per church in 1987 for the Oxford
Diocese and for the Church of England were respectively 80
and — quite fortuitously — 96.

Groups Within The Church

Three indicators of the spiritual life of a church are the
crèche, the young people's group, and the adult bible-
study/discussion group. A regular Sunday School or crèche
was held at three fifths of the churches. The situation at
those churches is shown below.

Church crèches

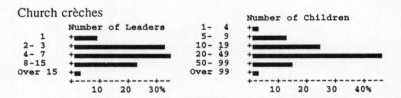

A third of the crèches had between two and three leaders, a
further third between four and seven. The average was four.
Just under half of the crèches had between 20 and 49
children, whilst a further quarter had between ten and
nineteen. The average was 28. A regular young people's
group was considerably less common, however, being held
at only a third of the churches.

Young people's groups

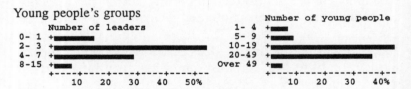

Slightly over half the groups had between two and three
leaders. The average was three. Membership seemed to be
smaller than that of crèches, in addition to there being fewer
of them. The average was nineteen.

A regular adult Bible-study or Christian discussion group
was more common than a crèche, taking place at, or being

available to, members of three fifths of the churches taking part in the survey.

Bible study groups

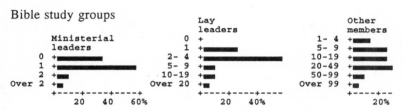

Roughly a third of the groups met without a ministerial leader. In some cases he/she attended, but not as a leader. Over half the groups had between two and four lay leaders; the average was four. It is perhaps reassuring that not a single group was without some measure of lay leadership. A priest discouraging lay leadership of this form might also be unwilling to delegate responsibility to others such as, for example, the musical director. There would appear to be a reasonably high level of general participation in these events, the average number of non-leaders being 26.

Although church policy is normally decided by the PCC, there may be subcommittees reporting to it. These may include a worship committee and/or one specifically to consider music. A quarter of churches taking part in the survey had a worship committee. It would have been interesting to know whether clergy would in general be in favour of such a group; the presence of one suggests an openness in decision making. However, less than one church in ten had a working group devoted to music. Again it is unclear whether clergy and/or musical directors would be hostile to such an idea. Perhaps they could see nothing to be gained by the presence of such a group, or possibly no-one would be prepared to serve on it, or even simply no-one had thought of it.

The Choir

The music or worship committees may *discuss* the music, but it is the choir that actually has to take the lead in singing it. I asked both parties whether there was a regular choir, drawing their attention to the definition that had been adopted (page 81). According to the clergy, 55% of churches had a choir: the musical directors reported 60%.[1] Four out of five choirs were robed rather than unrobed.

Number of members of choir

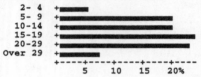

The average number of members per choir was sixteen (seven male, nine female); for the same choirs three years earlier (i.e. excluding those that had since disbanded) the figure had been fifteen. Here at least, the status quo had been maintained. However, for every 100 choirs in existence at the time of the survey, there had three years earlier been 114 according to the musical directors, 109 according to the clergy. This represents a substantial reduction in so short a time.

The average size of choir found by Hill[2] in 1982 at RSCM churches was 22, compared with the sixteen found here. This too implies a reduction in choir strength since 1982,[3] although it may simply be the effect of the differing types of church in the two surveys. Hill compares his own findings for the relative proportions of boys, girls, men and women with those cited in Temperley[4], which in turn had been taken from Reports of the Chief Commissioner of the School of English Church Music (now RSCM). I have extended Hill's table to include the corresponding figures

---

[1] Since the clergy figures included those churches where there was no musical director and, by implication, no choir either, the agreement seems reasonable.
[2] Berkeley Hill, *A Survey of Church Music, 1982* (Royal School of Church Music, Addington, 1983), pp. 13, 20.
[3] On page 127 we look at evidence of an unusually large number of resignations of musical directors at about that time.
[4] Nicholas Temperley *The Music of the English Parish Church* (CUP, Cambridge, 1979), p. 337.

from my survey and those inferred from the ACCMUS statistical report.

COMPOSITION OF CHOIRS

Year	Boys %	Girls %	Men %	Women %	Sample size	Author
1951	54.7	2.7	29.1	13.5	244	SECM[1]
1982	24.5	24.5	25.7	25.4	1223	Hill
1988/9	19.2	28.7	22.6	29.5	108	Rees
1988	17.7	25.4	23.8	33.1	377	Cooper[2]

The proportion of males, and boys in particular, seems to be continuing to decline. One might ask to what extent this decline is being caused by admitting girls into a previously all-male choir (a source of contention already noted on page 11). So how is the traditional all-male choir faring? Seven were reported in the survey, some 6% of the total. Their average membership figure was 19, compared with 16 for choirs as a whole, so in this respect the all-male choir was doing well. Closer inspection of the data, however, suggests a less healthy situation. One choir had shown significant growth, two had shown little change, whilst four had significantly declined. Subject to the caveat of limited data, the all-male choir therefore seems to be on the wane.

[1] Reports of the SECM Chief Commissioner, *English Church Music 20* (September–November 1949), p. 14; *20* (December 1949–February 1950), p. 35; *22* (June–November 1951), p. 10; *22* (December 1951–February 1952), p. 63.

[2] Jacqui Cooper, *Music in Parish Worship* (Central Board of Finance of the Church of England, London, [dated] 1990 [but not published until 1992]), pp. 28–29. (Cooper's figures include those in singing groups as well as those in choirs.)

To what extent are choirs an aging population?

Age distribution of choir members[1]

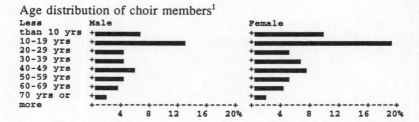

The age group of highest membership, for both males and females, is 10–19, followed by the under-tens. Membership falls away in the twenties, possibly as a result of leaving home and setting up one's own, but picks up a little in middle age. I wonder why this renewal of interest seems more pronounced for women than for men — the former returning after having had children, while the latter are still developing their career perhaps? There is then a gradual decline. Only in the highest age range do males (marginally) exceed females. This may be because the male voice seems to 'wear' better with age. An alternative explanation may be that the singing careers of those over 70 would in many cases have begun in the days when all-male choirs were much more common, resulting in a disproportionate number of men at the top of the scale. The average age of the males was 31, that of females 29.

On page 161 I assess the levels of ability of choirs according to the anthems that they were reported as singing. One choir in seven did not hold practices at all.

The traditional seating position of the choir has in certain quarters given rise to accusations of elitism. In other cases, the choir is simply so far away from the congregation that it cannot be heard. I therefore asked whether the choir sat close to the congregation, or apart (for example in the chancel or gallery). Furthermore, the increasing use of nave altars can leave a chancel choir appearing to be isolated. Therefore in certain churches having the choir close to the

---

[1] Based on 1704 members in 108 choirs.

congregation may be beneficial. This arrangement was in operation in just over a third of those churches with choirs. I also wanted to know whether the seating arrangement had recently changed — it certainly had. In as short a space as three years, one choir in eleven had been moved. In all cases but one, the move had been such that the choir was now located near the congregation. It would have been interesting to know whether the moves had the whole-hearted co-operation of the choirs in question, and whether in retrospect the moves had been generally perceived as beneficial. However, limits on the size of the questionnaires prevented investigation of these questions. Although the reasons for bringing the choir to the congregation may be strong and in accord with current thinking on worship, other factors such as the church architecture, acoustics, and 'visibility' between choir and organist, may sometimes make the matter less clear-cut than it might at first appear.

The financial aspects, from a church's point of view, of running a choir will be considered on page 132. However, weddings often provide external income for the members of the choir, quite apart from the additional opportunities for singing. I asked directors to specify the numbers of paid and unpaid weddings per year, both for adult members and for the child members. Just under two thirds of choirs included adults who sang at weddings at least occasionally. Of these, only a third were not paid, with one in five receiving payment for ten or more weddings per year. The total number of weddings (paid or unpaid) ranged from one to twenty: the average was six. Similarly, two thirds of choirs included children who sang at weddings at least occasionally. Unlike the adults, however, the children of only one in twelve choirs were not paid for weddings. On the other hand, more than a third received payment for ten or more weddings per year. The total number of weddings (paid or unpaid) attended by child choir members per year ranged from 1 to 81, with an average of eleven.

Although it is often the choir that derives the main benefit from affiliation to the Royal School of Church Music, this is strictly speaking held by the church. Some 42% of the churches were affiliated.

Summary

There is a reasonable amount of evidence to suggest that the churches involved in the survey are representative of the Church of England as a whole. Despite some disturbingly low electoral-roll figures and the absence of a young-people's group from two thirds of the churches, roughly three fifths were nonetheless able to sustain a crèche and/or adult study group.

Roughly one choir in eleven had disbanded in the three years preceding the survey, although the remaining choirs had been able to sustain their membership at around the sixteen level. A long-term fall in the numbers of boys in choirs appeared to be continuing and, as a particular example of this, there was evidence of difficulties in sustaining traditional all-male choirs.

5

He Who Would Valiant Be[1]

The Church and its Musical Director

After considering certain groups within the church, we now turn to someone who is — or should be — one of its key members. What exactly is the role of the musical director?

We look at the circumstances surrounding the original appointment, and investigate the frequency with which musical directors and priests come and go. We encounter the financial aspects of the work, namely his/her own salary, the budget for new music, and the expenses associated with running a choir. We consider also the extent to which the musical director determines musical policy.

Comings and Goings

First, how is a musical director recruited?

How did you hear of the post of musical director?

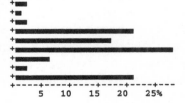

```
Ch. Times / Ch. of Eng. Newspaper
A music periodical
Other press
A friend
As asst. organist / choir member
As a member of the congregation
Mus. dir. is priest-in-charge
Mus. dir. is asst. priest
Other
                                 5    10   15   20   25%
```

---

[1] John Bunyan et al, [in, for example,] *The English Hymnal* (New Edition) (OUP and Mowbray, London, 1933), No. 402.

Less than one in twenty of the musical directors had been
recruited by external advertisement. The largest single
recruitment area seemed to be the congregational pews —
almost twice as common as the choir stalls — or from being
an apprentice to the predecessor. This could imply an
element of arm-twisting in the appointment. I mentioned on
page 86 those in the seventh category, the priest-in-charge,
but the assistant priests made an unexpected group. Had
there been more of them, a comparison with lay musical
directors would have made an interesting study. Many of
those in the 'other' category were approached by the church;
others were or had been organist at another church, and were
approached via their own vicar.

Next I wanted to discover the fierceness of competition for
these posts.

Was there more than one suitable candidate for the post
of musical director?

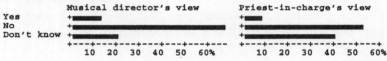

It is perhaps surprising that there was a higher percentage of
'don't know' responses amongst the clergy as employers
than amongst the directors as employees. This may be
caused by the director having been at the church longer than
the priest, or the fact that the director would take a greater
interest in the subject. However it is clear that both parties
agreed that there had been more than one suitable candidate
in only a very few cases — one in six in the view of the
directors, worse than one in seven in the view of the clergy.
Such figures could have serious implications for the avail-
ability of the next generation of musical directors. One of
the directors was magnanimous enough to admit that there
had been another suitable candidate — her husband.

When asking the musical director how long he/she had
been in post, I felt it only fair to ask the priest-in-charge the
same question.

For how many years have you been at this church?

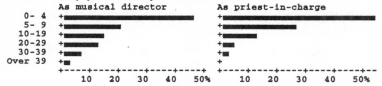

Whilst a third of the directors had held their post for more than ten years, only a fifth of clergy had done so. The averages were 10.2 and 7.0 years respectively. Although an average figure for organists was not given in Hill's 1982 survey,[1] I estimate it to have been 9.6, remarkably close to the figure of 10.2 found here. In the occasional leaflet *Parish and People*, edited by a group of clergy in the Oxford Diocese, the following text appears:

> *The Minister & the Organist — A Study in Role Conflict* could be the title for a post-graduate's thesis. To begin with, a survey would be likely to reveal that the organist has seen the back of several vicars (not only at the altar) — seemingly he goes on for ever. His seat on the organ stool is more permanent than that of the man with the 'real actual and corporeal possession of the vicarage'. The parson may have his freehold, but the organist may have a stranglehold on the parish.[2]

These are strong words, no doubt written from bitter personal experience. However, there is a simple explanation of this situation. In the course of their professional working lives, both priest and musical director may expect to move from one job to another, not infrequently through promotion. In the case of the director, unless there is associated with the job change a geographical relocation as well, there is no intrinsic reason why he/she will not be able to continue as director at the same church. On the other hand, a change of job for a priest almost always involves a change of church. It is therefore only to be expected that the turnover of clergy

[1] Berkeley Hill, *A Survey of Church Music, 1982* (Royal School of Church Music, Addington, 1983), p. 41.

[2] 'The Lost Accord' in *Parish and People*, 27 (1986), [p. 2].

will be faster than that of musical directors. Indeed, a larger differential than that actually found would not have been entirely surprising.

With the words of *Parish and People* still ringing in our ears, we must now start to tread more warily as we enter slightly more dangerous territory.

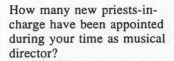

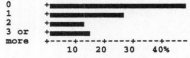

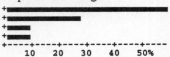

Just under half the directors had always served the same priest-in-charge at their present church. However, since more directors had witnessed the appointment of three or more new priests than had witnessed the appointment of two, it seems reasonable to infer that a significant proportion had seen the arrival of four or more. At well over half the churches, the current priest-in-charge had never appointed a new musical director. It then seemed sensible to compare individuals' length of service with the number of new appointments of their 'other half'. Naturally, in general the number of new appointments of the other half depended on how long an individual had been at the church. However, there were some exceptions in the form of longstanding partnerships: one musical director had served only two priests in over 29 years' service, and a certain priest had needed to appoint only two musical directors in over 39 years. More worrying were the cases of the musical directors who had seen the arrival (and by inference the departure) of at least three priests-in-charge in less than ten years, and the priest who had needed to appoint four new musical directors in the same period.

I also wanted to know how many years' experience each director had acquired before taking up the present appointment. I was then able to obtain an approximate measure of the *total* number of years' experience as a musical director, by combining the figures in the left-hand chart with the number of years' service at his/her present church. The result is shown in the right-hand chart. (The assumption that no significant further time was spent as musical director at a third church is probably valid in most cases — especially in view of the high proportion of musical directors who had never held another appointment at all.)

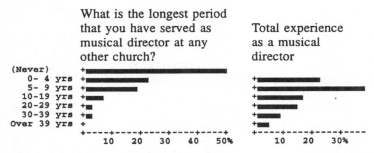

At slightly over half the churches, this was their musical director's first appointment, and at only one church in nine had a director been appointed who already held ten or more years' experience. The total experience of well over half of the musical directors was less than ten years (the average was 13), a surprisingly short period in view of the fact that as many as one in twenty of the directors had accumulated some forty years' experience. Moreover, Hill's survey[1] only a few years earlier revealed significantly higher total lengths of service, the average then being 17 years. We must not draw any hasty conclusions. However, we cannot escape the fact that a particularly large number of directors took up their first appointment less than ten years before the present survey (1988–89), presumably to replace others who had resigned. We have already noted that *The Alternative Service Book* was published in 1980.

---

[1] Berkeley Hill, *A Survey of Church Music, 1982* (Royal School of Church Music, Addington, 1983), p. 41.

Finally in this section we turn to the question of contracts. Much has been written in recent years extolling the benefits of giving the musical director a written contract.

> The Royal College of Organists' contract has now been superseded by a more detailed and comprehensive document subject to the provisions of Canon B20.[1] . . . [It] has been issued on the authority of the Incorporated Association of Organists, the Incorporated Society of Musicians, the RSCM, and the Legal Adviser to the General Synod. [It had also the authority of the RCO, although for some reason this was not stated.] Whether or not organists do in fact have a contract as of now, we strongly urge all concerned to enter into this new agreement which we believe to be much more satisfactory than the old one and in the best interests of all parties.[2]

> The Legal Advisory Commission of the General Synod has advised that it is essential for the appointment of an organist to be subject to an agreement in writing which must reflect the present law in regard to appointment and dismissal. It is important for the sake of a satisfactory understanding on both sides for this advice to be heeded and we recommend that all organists . . . insist on the terms of their appointment being confirmed in writing.[3]

Furthermore, respondents to an Administry survey reported that giving the musical director a written job description removed a number of 'pockets of confusion and unease'.[4] I wondered what was happening in practice.

What is the nature of your present contract as musical director?

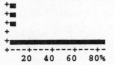

```
'Local' written; non-fixed term   +■
'Local' written; fixed term       +■
Standard written; non-fixed term  +■
Standard written; fixed term      +
No written contract               +■■■■■■■■■■■■■■■■■■
                                  +---+---+---+---+-
                                   20  40  60  80%
```

[1] See page 108.
[2] Lionel Dakers 'A revised form of agreement for organists and choir directors' in *Church Music Quarterly*, January 1987, p. 13.
[3] *Organists' Guide to Employment*, (Incorporated Society of Musicians, London, 1990), p. 1.
[4] *A Joyful Noise*, (Resource Paper 84:7), (Administry, St Albans, 1984), p. 6.

Only one in six of the musical directors had any form of written contract. However, we must allow the last word (so to speak) to the director whose description of her contract was simply: 'Until death!'.

Matters of Finance

Closely associated with contracts are matters financial, in which the director of music is likely to be involved at least to some extent, for example his/her own salary, the budget for new music, and the expenses associated with running a choir. (There will also be the expenses of organ maintenance, but we will not consider these further here.)

I asked directors to state their annual salary, including expenses where applicable but excluding fees, offered to them. The question was so phrased because directors often refuse to accept some or all of their nominal salary. Despite this, the high incidence of the figure zero suggests that the question was answered by many in terms of salary received rather than salary offered. We may, however, be confident that the salary received was not greater than the figures in the table. (Assistant priests serving as musical director were excluded from the data.) The salary for two fifths of the posts was zero, whilst for only about a fifth was it greater than £500. The average (excluding one exceptionally high salary[1] of £9800) was £282. One director reported receiving no payment, but conceded that he received 'an ex gratia capon at Christmas'. From the salary and data in other parts of the questionnaire I next estimated the payment per attendance[2].

---

[1] This particular post included considerable pastoral responsibility.

[2] I arbitrarily assumed that: if the director was involved in N services per month, after allowance for holidays, this would amount to 11 x N services per year; also, if choir practices were held, the director would be involved in 45 practices per year, a total of (11 x N) + 45 attendances.

Payment offered to musical directors

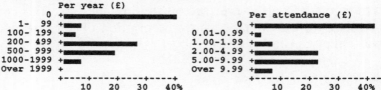

If the director was offered payment at all, it was most unlikely to be less than £2.00 or more than £10.00 per attendance. The wide variation, namely a factor of five, almost certainly represents not only the differences in skills required for different appointments, but also the varying financial strengths of individual churches. Both parties were asked their views on the adequacy of the director's salary. Many did not directly answer this question, but simply wrote the word 'voluntary' beside it. One director went further and wrote: 'I don't think church musicians should be paid'.

Views on adequacy of payment offered to musical directors

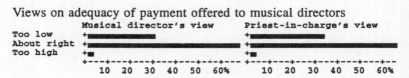

There was remarkable consistency in the views of the two parties, with almost a third feeling that the salary was too low. One director who ticked the 'about right' box added: 'It is right because obviously the church cannot afford more, but in worldly terms it's senseless'. Another, ticking the same box, added that it would be far too low for anyone relying on the income. Another stated that his salary had been unchanged for six years, but it could, if he asked, be increased. Then were added the words: 'Yes I will!'. I next examined the directors' perceptions of the adequacy of their salary in terms of the salary itself. (The post at £9800 was excluded from this particular study, although in fact both parties at that church felt the salary to be about right.)

PAYMENT OFFERED TO MUSICAL DIRECTORS
COMPARED WITH THEIR PERCEPTIONS OF ITS ADEQUACY

	Average annual payment	Average payment per attendance
'Too low'	£280	£3.00
'About right'	£300	£3.24
'Too high'	£265	£6.00

An increase of less than 10% seemed to be sufficient to change directors' feelings on salary from inadequacy to adequacy, and we may conclude that the difference was more of attitudes than the level of payment itself. The results where the payment was perceived to be too high are based on only two appointments of considerably differing nature, and should be treated with caution. In an earlier question (page 105), musical directors were invited to give their views on various criteria that a director might apply in deciding whether to accept a church appointment, ranging from 1 (very advantageous), through 2 (advantageous), 3 (not relevant), and so on. The average figure of those who felt that their present salary was too low was 2.20, compared with 2.58 for all the others. Therefore, those who felt their present salary was too low were more concerned about salary in general. This would seem to confirm the view that perception of adequacy of salary depends more on the attitude of the individual than on the level of payment.

In its survey of church music, Administry found contrasting views on the paying of church musicians:[1]

Why should organists be paid sums of money? We don't pay Sunday School teachers, treasurers or churchwardens. We expect these people to offer their time and talents free.

A full- or part-time salaried music director can give real vision to a church because he has time to plan, and seek God's face on this matter. I feel that in a larger church, a salaried music director is a *must* — the Bible lays stress in this area (see 1 Chronicles [6:31-32]); so should we.

---

[1] *A Joyful Noise* (Resource Paper 84:7), (Administry, St. Albans, 1984), p. 6.

Less controversial, although perhaps no easier to find, will be the funds for new music for a church. While a quarter of churches spent over £100 annually on this, nearly a half spent less than £5. In many cases, therefore, either no music at all was being introduced or some illicit photocopying was taking place. Equally revealing was the budget per member of the electoral roll.

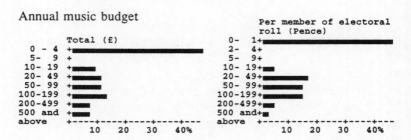

At almost half the churches, the annual expenditure was less than two pence per member of the electoral roll, a truly appalling situation. To take an example, a church buying a replacement set of hymn books might, with a grant from the publishers, have expected at the time of the survey to pay around £3 per words-only book. On this basis, the new set would take the entire music budget for the next 300 years!

Another item on the accounts will be the expenses of running the choir. The children were paid at two fifths of the churches, the adults at only one in fifty. The paying of certain children and not others was very rare indeed, and did not occur at all in the case of adults. This is unlike some churches, notably in London, where a professional quartet forms the core of an otherwise volunteer choir. I asked whether the choir initiated its own fund-raising and, if so, whether it had full control over the funds. This question raises several issues. From the point of view of the church treasurer, a choir is a source of expense, however beautiful its sound may be. If the choir is enthusiastic it will be wanting to buy new music and, if robed, there is also the expense of maintaining the robes. Does the choir attempt to cover these expenses or does it believe that its enriching of the church's worship is contribution enough? Over three quarters of the choirs did not undertake their own fund-raising (despite generous contributions perhaps from individual members). By implication, they were not corporately contributing to church funds either. It is possible that, if they did, expressions of resentment sometimes heard against choirs, especially in evangelical circles, might be dispelled. One director, however, reported that the choir did indeed assist in raising general church funds. Of the remaining choirs that did undertake fund-raising, two thirds had full control of the funds. Of those that did not, there were instances of choir members feeling resentful at 'their' money being controlled by non-members (for example, the parochial church council). However, this in turn would cause concern within the church that the choir apparently saw itself as an autonomous body wishing to be outside the normal decision-making processes. At one church where the choir did not undertake fund-raising, the musical director commented: 'I am also the church treasurer!'.

Matters of Policy

Before turning our attention to matters of specifically musical policy, let us look at the church's official decision-making body, namely the parochial church council, and the role that the musical director may or may not play within it.

In these days of increasing lay involvement, few people qualify more for inclusion on the PCC than the organist. Furthermore the opportunity which his presence provides for deepening the relationship and understanding between him, the incumbent, the churchwardens and the other parishioners can be of great benefit to the life of the church — and prevent those misunderstandings which all too often appear in the press.[1]

---

[1] Nigel McCulloch (Archdeacon of Sarum, quoted by Lionel Dakers), 'From the Director', *Church Music Quarterly*, April 1983, p. 3.

The tradition that an organist who is an employee should not be a member of the PCC is an unhelpful one.[1]

So I asked the directors:

Are you, as musical director, a member of the PCC?

```
Yes, ex officio as mus. dir. +▬
Yes, in some other capacity +▬▬▬▬▬▬▬
No                          +▬▬▬▬▬▬▬▬▬▬▬▬▬▬▬▬▬▬▬▬▬▬▬
                            +---+---+---+---+---+---+--
                            10  20  30  40  50  60%
```

In only one church in twenty was the director a member of PCC (or its equivalent) ex officio. In only a third was he/she on the PCC at all. This seems rather discouraging. In particular, I wondered whether the response of one director: 'No, thank God' was perhaps the private view of many others. In half of the churches, the musical director had never been invited to serve on the PCC. This too is disappointing, since it suggests a lack of desire on the part of others that the director become involved in anything other than purely musical responsibilities.

When I asked the clergy and musical directors whether they felt that in general musical directors should be a member of the PCC ex officio, the clergy were equally split for and against, with one in six undecided. The directors were marginally more in favour, namely three out of five, with one third against, and the remainder undecided. Neither party therefore was particularly keen: some clergy may possibly look upon the musical director as a rival, whilst the director may see the PCC as one of the 'other church activities' for which there was no great enthusiasm (page 102).

I wondered to what extent the director was allowed to play his/her part in determining the church's musical policy, especially in the light of the following comment.

---

[1] *In Tune With Heaven*, Report of the Archbishops' Commission on Church Music (Church House Publishing, and Hodder and Stoughton, London, 1992), p. 245.

In an ideal situation the choice and use of hymns is a matter of joint concern and a joint responsibility, something which should apply to all aspects of the work of clergy and musicians.[1]

So I asked:

Who generally chooses the congregational hymns/songs?[2]

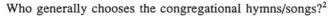
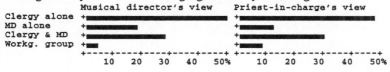

There was general agreement that the priest-in-charge was solely responsible for the choice of hymns in about half of the churches. The musical director was solely responsible in roughly one seventh of cases, and some sort of corporate decision was taken in the remainder. The musical directors need in no way feel aggrieved over this relative absence of decision-making on their part: a priest may wish to devote a service to a specific theme, and choose the hymns accordingly. In any case, choosing hymns carefully is a very time-consuming task! Let us reserve judgment for the moment. A survey undertaken by Administry[3] reported four other ways of selecting hymns. These were: 'Songs of Praise' services (as in the television programme, the person choosing the hymn explains the reasons for the choice); choices in advance (via a 'favourite hymns' box); spontaneous choices from the congregation (although other churches in the same survey pointed out that this negated the objectivity of liturgical worship); and spontaneous leadership from the congregation (in which a member can start a song on the spur of the moment — this was not felt to be suitable aesthetically in other than the merest handful of cases; there could also be problems of pitch).

[1] Lionel Dakers, *Choosing and Using Hymns* (Mowbray, London, 1985), p. 4.
[2] In this and the following two questions, I have excluded from the musical directors' data those priests-in-charge who were acting as their own musical director.
[3] *A Joyful Noise*, (Resource Paper 84:7), (Administry, St Albans, 1984), p. 8.

Next I asked:

Who generally chooses the tunes for these hymns/songs?

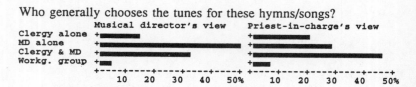

There seems to be considerably less agreement over who chooses the tunes. It is perhaps surprising, and certainly less than satisfactory, that the clergy seem to be in total control in as many as about one case in six. Given the small number of working groups for music or for worship (page 117), it is not surprising that they seem to play so limited a part. Respondents may well have had difficulty deciding which of two boxes to tick. For example, a musical director might actually choose a tune, but informally ask the priest for his agreement. The director would therefore tick the second box, the priest the third.

Finally in this group of questions I asked:

Who generally chooses all the other music sung at regular services?

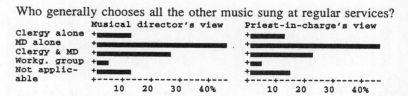

There was clear agreement that, in just under half of the churches, the musical director was given full control over the other music and, in about half of the remaining cases, the decision was a joint one. However, at one church in ten, the clergy had full jurisdiction. I find this unsatisfactory, and wonder whether the directors did not wish to take part in the decision-making or were simply not allowed to. Alternatively, however, the director and priest might be of such a single mind on matters musical that there would be no need for the former to be consulted at all. Was this really so?

Have the musical director and priest-in-charge an agreed policy
on music in worship?

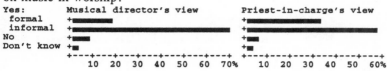

It is encouraging that nine out of ten of both parties felt that
they had an agreed policy with their 'other half' on the use
of music in worship. However, the size of the discrepancy
between the figures on *formal* agreement is a little surprising. In some of the churches where the parties did not know
whether they agreed, one or other of them had only recently
arrived. In the others, I hope that the parties subsequently
gave the matter some thought. Perhaps they even got around
to discussing it!

This brings us to a related matter. Do the musical director
and priest work as a team or independently of each other?
As a pointer to this, I asked them about the meetings held
between them.

How often do the musical director and priest-in-charge hold meetings
to discuss the music?[1]

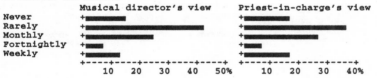

At just over half the churches, meetings either did not take
place at all or at best took place only rarely. However, at no
fewer than two thirds of the churches where the response
was 'never', the musical director would welcome one. In the
case of the priests-in-charge the figure was even higher, at
three quarters. Perhaps I ought to have written to the priest

---

[1]   It was of course necessary to exclude, from both the priests' data and the
      musical directors', those priests-in-charge who served as their own musical
      director.

and musical director at those churches where both wanted to hold meetings, but had never done so!

How long is a typical meeting?

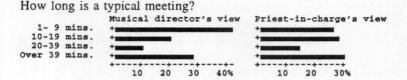

There was some disagreement over the length of meetings, in particular the first two categories, probably because any meetings roughly 10 minutes long could equally well fit into either category. However, there was a good measure of agreement over the average duration, namely 21 minutes estimated from the musical directors' figures, and 24 from those of the clergy. One director complained that the normal 'meeting' comprised being given the hymn list on a scrap of paper three minutes before the service. On the other hand, one priest asked whether the time was inclusive or exclusive of drinks.

Total time spent per year in meetings between musical director and priest-in-charge

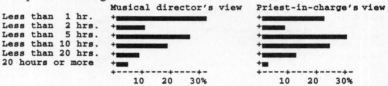

I estimated the total time spent per year in meetings between the two parties by combining the previous two sets of results.[1] Given the uncertainties, the charts are reasonably similar. The averages were 5.3 and 5.5 hours from the musical directors' figures and those of the clergy respectively — consistent but depressingly low. Moreover, these figures do not include the cases where there was no meeting at all.

---

[1]   The figure for the range 'over 39 minutes' was arbitrarily chosen to be 45. Particularly difficult was 'rarely', which was equally arbitrarily chosen to be three times per year.

If, however, these cases *are* included, we are confronted by even bleaker figures. According to the musical directors, there was either no meeting at all, or the total annual duration was an hour or less, at more than two fifths of the churches. According to the clergy, it was more than a third. In other words, at such churches there seems to be virtually no communication between clergy and musical director of even a semi-formal nature. Indeed it is arguable whether a discussion lasting 'between one and nine minutes', constitutes a formal meeting at all.

In those cases where a priest-in-charge is sharing pastoral responsibility, 'staff meetings' often take place weekly, with a total annual duration of 100 hours or more. The times spent with musical directors contrast sharply with such a figure. In many cases not only does the priest not have any assistant, he also has to spread himself over several churches. It is therefore all the more distressing that clearly the musical director is not seen as a colleague with whom matters, not necessarily of a directly pastoral nature, can be discussed.

How helpful do you find these meetings?

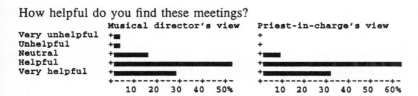

Apart from the few unfortunate directors in the first two categories, the overall forms of the charts are similar and indeed encouraging. One priest did not answer the question directly, but simply wrote 'necessary' against it. One musical director confessed to finding the question difficult to answer, since the priest-in-charge was her husband.

Meetings of a different sort were in my mind when I formulated the next question. While the draft questionnaires were being circulated to senior church musicians and clergy for their comments, one of them received a letter of appeal from an organist who felt that his vicar was trying to spy on him. The vicar's presence at every choir practice was proving intolerable. In the production questionnaires, I therefore asked directors to specify which of the following statements most closely described the situation at their choir practice (if there was one):

• priest-in-charge does not regularly attend and would not be welcome;
• he/she does not regularly attend but would be welcome;
• he/she regularly attends and is not welcome;
• he/she regularly attends and is welcome.

Whatever other problems may have been besetting the musical directors taking part in the survey, this was not one of them — no-one at all voted for the third option. The director at one church in ten would not welcome the clergy's presence if he/she appeared, but six times as many would. At one church in seven, the priest regularly attended practices and was welcome. In short, most directors saw nothing wrong in the priest attending, an indication of a satisfactory working relationship. Returning to the case of the distressed organist, it is surprising that the vicar found time to attend choir practice but, given the fact that he did, perhaps his intentions were being entirely misinterpreted.

Multiple or Shared Responsibilities

I asked: 'For how many churches, including this one, are you responsible?'[1] Very few were directors of music at

---

[1] This question appeared also in the clergy questionnaire. I asked it partly as a check: if a group of questionnaires from the same respondent became accidentally separated, they could be reunited. However, despite my underlining the word 'including', it was clear from the number of 'zero' responses that some had answered the question as if it had read 'excluding'. The *Oxford Diocesan Year Book 1988* (Oxford Diocesan Board of Finance, Oxford, 1987) enabled me to discover the extent of this confusion — at least amongst the clergy. Only a quarter of the churches were in the care of a priest without pastoral responsibilities elsewhere, whilst almost half were in the care of one with responsibilities at two or more other churches. Such is the shortage of clergy and such is the pastoral load that they must bear. For a priest to be in charge of six churches (and have to attend six PCC meetings instead of one!) is surely far too much of a burden. Overall, the level of

more than one church although, if the national shortage of organists continues, this will have to change, or more churches will be without 'live' music altogether. One of the respondents merits special mention as both musical director *and* priest-in-charge at no fewer than four churches.

Unless a choir is very competent, it ideally needs to be conducted, and this is of course not possible in accompanied works without an assistant. So I asked: 'Do you have at this church an assistant musical director who *regularly* shares responsibility with you either as choirmaster or organist?' The word 'regular' was emphasised in order to exclude what might be termed 'holiday-locum' organists. At one church in three there was an unsalaried assistant, but at only one in fourteen a salaried one. At almost three churches out of five, there was no regular assistant at all.[1]

Summary

Musical directors tended to remain in post at a church somewhat longer than the priest-in-charge. However, the number of musical directors with long periods of experience, either in their current church or elsewhere, was unexpectedly small. Very few directors had any written contract. In still fewer cases was there more than one suitable candidate when the director was appointed.

Where a fee was offered at all to a musical director, £2 per visit (including choir practice, if any) was typical.

---

clergy misinterpretation of the question was very low, and it would seem almost an insult to the collective intelligence of musical directors to suggest that the proportion of them misinterpreting the question was significantly greater.

[1] I excluded from these figures the special cases of the churches where the priests-in-charge saw themselves also as musical director. In three fifths of these cases there was some sort of 'assistant' who probably better fitted our definition of musical director. Whether that person was unwilling or unable to complete the questionnaire, or why the priest was unwilling for him/her to do so, we will never know. At the remainder there was no assistant. The picture of an already overworked clergyman darting between pulpit, lectern *and* organ console is therefore not quite as common as we might at first have feared.

However a clear majority were satisfied with their rate of pay. A typical annual budget for new music at a church was only £10.

Rarely was the director on the PCC ex officio. Hymns tended to be chosen by the clergy, whilst the musical director had at least a major say in the choice of tunes and, where applicable, even more influence in the choice of any other music. Although there was usually some sort of 'understanding' between the priest and musical director on the role of music in worship, they devoted very little time actually to discussing it. Where meetings were not currently taking place, a majority of both parties nonetheless expressed the wish that they should. Where meetings were taking place, both parties usually found them helpful.

At two fifths of the churches there was an assistant musical director on a regular basis.

6

Come, Let Us Join
Our Cheerful Songs[1]

The Church and its Music in Worship

So far we have been looking at the backgrounds and general attitudes of clergy and musical directors, and their perceptions of what was happening overall at their churches. Now we come to more controversial matters — the services and, more particularly, the music in them.

I was seeking answers to a number of questions. For example, how often could we expect to encounter a service with music at a given church? How many people would we find there? Would the music be 'ancient' or 'modern'? Ditto the liturgy, and would the emphasis of worship best be caricatured as 'bells and smells' or 'happy-clappy'?

Jerusalem is built as a city that is at unity in itself.[2] Could the same be said of the words and the music in the service, the music and the musical resources, and — especially — the priest-in-charge and the musical director?

Both parties were invited to provide information on up to three different types of service with music regularly taking place at their churches. Although we will be mainly examining the music, we look first at the more general questions relating to these services.

---

[1] H. Lahee, [in, for example,] *The English Hymnal* (OUP and Mowbray, London, 1906), No. 376.
[2] *Psalm 122*, v. 3 (*BCP*).

The Worship

Although we need to ask questions about the worship and its participants, first of all we must discover when the service with music is actually being held. Are we even safe in assuming that all such services are held on Sunday? Whilst said communion services on weekdays are not at all unknown, I was unaware of the existence of weekday services with music (other than in cathedrals and collegiate foundations). I was right: with the exception of a weekday eucharist with hymns at a couple of churches, and a weekly mothers' and toddlers' service at a further two, all the regular services with music took place on a Sunday. Few churches, however, offered a *choice* of musical services on any given Sunday: at just over two fifths there was on average only one such service per week, while at a further quarter it took place even less frequently. As many as two fifths of the services had already begun by 10.15 a.m. — presumably to allow the rest of Sunday for recreation.

What type of service could we expect to encounter? Not surprisingly, the musical director and the priest-in-charge were in close agreement on this.

Liturgy

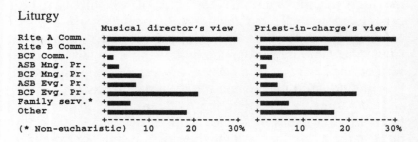

(* Non-eucharistic)

Just under half the services were communion-based.[1] The most common liturgy was Rite A, followed by *BCP* Evening Prayer. 'Other' comprised services no longer in widespread use, for example Series 2 communion, and hybrids such as morning prayer and communion in the same service.

---

[1] These tables of course exclude any said services.

The liturgy of the Church of England can mean all things to all men, and the above tables provide no information on the *style* of worship. I therefore also requested information on the services' degree of charismatic worship, and their catholic or evangelical emphasis. When on page 99 we looked at the personal preferences in worship of both parties, we noted a lower response rate than in other questions. A similar reduction occurred here.

Degree of charismatic worship in services

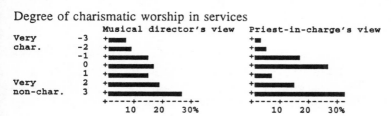

The averages for musical director and clergy were respectively 0.8 and 1.0 (i.e. verging slightly towards non-charismatic). Inevitably the grading of charismatic worship is subjective, nonetheless in three cases out of five where the question was answered by both parties, they were within one point of each other in their assessments. Most churches seem to be either middle-of-the-road, or strongly non-charismatic. Making use of the data shown on page 100, I examined the extent to which each party felt out of sympathy with the charismatic content of the worship taking place at the church. For three quarters of the directors responding, the church's approach to charismatic worship came to within one point of their personal preference. One director in ten indicated a difference of three points or greater, implying either significant dissatisfaction, or an error in understanding or answering the questions. Similar figures were found for the clergy. A priest, however, has the power to angle the services towards his own viewpoint while the director does not. The fact that a priest may choose not to do so will in all probability be to accommodate the specific church's requirements (of which he would presumably have been told before accepting the appointment). A deviation of three points or greater should not therefore necessarily be seen as a source of dissatisfaction in the way that it might be for a musical director.

Degree of catholic/evangelical worship in services

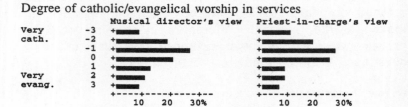

The averages for musical directors and clergy were respectively -0.2 and -0.5 (i.e. slightly catholic, the priests' perception being marginally more so). Again there is good agreement: in four cases out of five where the question was answered by both parties, they were within one point of each other in their assessments. The fact that there was a greater measure of agreement than in the case of charismatic/non-charismatic, is probably because the catholic/evangelical divide is more clearly recognised. For four fifths of the directors responding, their perception of the church's degree of catholic/evangelical worship came to within one point of their personal preference. One director in twelve indicated a difference of three points or greater, as before implying either significant dissatisfaction, or an error in understanding or answering the questions. Again the clergy figures were very similar, here also a large deviation should not necessarily be seen as a source of dissatisfaction.

The Worship and its Participants

Next we look at the participants attending these services. At just over half the churches, the size of congregation, excluding choir, at the *best-attended* of the services was less than 50 and, at one church in six, less than 20. The minimum and maximum were respectively 5 and 600, the average being 63. The total number of attendances at each church per month was also calculated. The average figure for this was 293, the minimum and maximum being 5 and 5160, an enormous range.

At more than nine tenths of the services reported, there was 'always/nearly always' an organist, and at a further one in twenty there was 'sometimes' one. Although this may seem encouraging, a word of caution is necessary: the question would fail to reveal a service which had become entirely said because an organist was no longer available. One priest remarked sadly: 'Unfortunately the organist can only be an occasional treat.' A pianist can be used instead of, or in addition to an organist. However, at only one service in 20 was a pianist 'always/nearly always' present: at a further service in seven one was 'sometimes' present.

The use of non-keyboard instrumentalists was slightly more widespread than that of pianists ('always/nearly always' at one service in 25, 'sometimes' at one in five). This is perhaps because different skills and hence different people are involved, and because the pianist will in many cases tend to be guided towards the organ console. Information on the nature of the instruments was requested, but not always provided. Sometimes the information was limited to 'instrumental group', but at least this implied a range of talents being used. In the following list, the instruments (or groups of instruments) are given in decreasing order of usage: guitar (by far the most common), flute, instrumental group, recorder, string group, clarinet, electronic keyboard, percussion group, brass group, orchestra, tape recorder (as a substitute for an organist), trumpet, woodwind group, digital horn, oboe. The percussion group at one church included bongo drums, highly effective no doubt, but possibly an acquired taste when used in the context of worship.

Next we turn to the choir, which on page 81 we arbitrarily defined as 'a group of singers (robed or unrobed) remaining *together* during a service, even when they are not singing'. It by no means unknown in some churches for the choir to outnumber the rest of the congregation. We looked earlier (page 118) at the size of choirs: now we see from the following tables that there would a roughly 50/50 chance of our encountering one at a service.

Choir present at services[1]

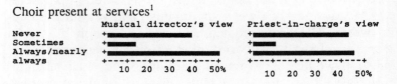

In some churches, especially those of a charismatic or evangelical outlook, music groups of a less formal nature have developed, sometimes being referred to as 'worship groups', and existing either alongside or instead of the traditional choir. (Choirs as such often seem to be regarded, rightly or wrongly, by these churches as elitist.) Adult singing groups seemed to find little place at those churches taking part in the survey ('never' 86%; 'sometimes' 10%; 'always/nearly always' 4%). In contrast, in a survey of mainly evangelical churches, singing groups were found in a third of the cases.[2] There seems to be no widely held definition which differentiates between 'choir' and 'worship group' (other than the type of music sung, the persuasion of the church, and possibly in which part of it the music is sung). We may, however, wish to take note of the following comment from a vicar of charismatic persuasion:

[1] The discrepancy between the two tables will have been caused by several factors. First, in those instances where the question was duplicated between questionnaires, and the priest-in-charge and director were one and the same person, the result was included only in a clergy capacity. In such a situation, a choir seems less likely than elsewhere. Other contributory factors included respondents intending a blank response to mean 'never', or the fact that the two sets of observations are not based on exactly the same set of churches. Finally, despite the note drawing respondents' attention to the definition of a choir within the questionnaire, there may have been minor confusion between it and any separate adult singing group.

[2] 'Results of Your Completed Questionnaire Forms' in *Music in Worship*, 39 (Summer 1987), p. 5.

It would be tragic if, within renewed worship, the worship group took on [the] negative traits previously belonging to the choir, yet in some places I can detect this happening in very small ways.[1]

Plus ça change?

At four fifths of the services reported, Sunday school choirs never sang (other than in perhaps a congregational capacity), and only 'sometimes' in almost all other cases. This is despite the fact that in doing so, the members of today might be encouraged to join — or even to form — the adult choir of tomorrow.

Other musicians did not seem to be widely utilised either ('never' 92%; 'sometimes' 7%; 'always/nearly always' 1%). These (together with the number of churches using them) were: solo singer 7, visiting choir 3, young people's singing group 1, mixed-age singing group 1, instrumental group 2, handbell ringers 1. (The last two groups were being used in their own right, either instead of or in addition to accompanying any singing. It would have been interesting to know the age ranges of these groups.) The director at one church reported that the priest-in-charge occasionally sang and accompanied himself on the guitar at family services. I could not resist checking to see whether they were one and the same person — they were not — but scrutiny of the questionnaire revealed a less than complimentary description of the standard of playing! I wonder whether the priest had ever considered asking someone else to play and/or sing — one or more of the older children perhaps?

The Worship and Its Music

We now turn to the specific subject of the music used in worship at the churches: hymns and congregational songs[2], psalms, settings of the eucharist, canticles, anthems, and other vocal music.

---

[1] John Leach, *Liturgy and Liberty* (MARC, Eastbourne, 1989), p. 82.
[2] The reason for using this composite term was explained on page 81.

Hymnals and Song Books

We examined earlier (pages 28–52) the centrality of hymnody in worship, and reviewed a number of the hymnals and song books in current use. The survey provided information not only on the relative usage of hymnals at each church, but also on their relative levels of acclaim by the two parties. Not surprisingly, multiple usage of hymnals was not at all uncommon. One church used no fewer than five in the same type of service, although the maximum number used on any one occasion was unclear. Whatever the figure, when combined perhaps with an *ASB* and a weekly leaflet, it must surely represent a formidable task for the sidesmen and women.[1]

Relative usage of hymn books

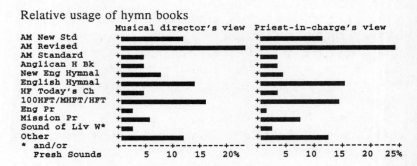

The leading position of *Ancient and Modern Revised* is likely to be increasingly overtaken by *Ancient and Modern New Standard*. Whilst some respondents may mistakenly have voted for the old *Standard* edition instead of one of the other two, the fact remains that it is still quite often to be seen in the pews of village churches. These three hymnals between them account for almost half the total usage. However, *The New English Hymnal*, published only two years before the distribution of the first questionnaires, was already making good headway. *Mission Praise* was rather

---

[1] Discrepancies between the observations of the two parties will partly have been caused by musical directors sometimes listing amongst their lesser-used hymnals those used for alternative tunes or harmonies.

more widespread than either *Anglican Hymn Book* or *Hymns for Today's Church*. Books listed in the 'other' category were, in decreasing order of usage: church's own compilation, *Celebration Hymnal, Songs of Fellowship, Come and Praise, Junior Praise, With One Voice* and seven others. One priest commented: 'overhead projector slides from all over the place'.

Ten years is a long time in relation to such surveys, but Hill[1] found that *Ancient and Modern Revised* was then being used as the main hymnal at 61% of churches, and as a supplementary hymnal at a further 10%. *100 Hymns for Today* was being used as a supplementary book at 80% of churches. *The English Hymnal* was being used as the main hymnal at 18% of churches, and as a supplementary book at 19%. *Ancient and Modern Standard* was the main book at 8%, and *Anglican Hymn Book* at 6%.

The questionnaire of the recent Archbishops' Commission sought information only on the recently published hymnals and on the numbers of churches in which they were being used (and without asking respondents to specify the degree of usage — in an extreme case the books could presumably stay for months at a time in a cupboard!). It found that *Mission Praise* or *Junior Praise* was used at more churches than *Ancient and Modern New Standard*.[2] This is confirmed in my own data — it is only when one considers relative levels of usage that the form of the charts on the previous page emerges. The Commission's statement that *Mission Praise* or *Junior Praise* were 'the most popular of all the hymn books listed in the questionnaire' is unfortunate not only for this reason, but also because the word 'popular' implies favour — which of course was not being measured.

---

[1] Berkeley Hill, *A Survey of Church Music, 1982* (Royal School of Church Music, Addington, 1983), pp. 54–55.

[2] *In Tune With Heaven*, Report of the Archbishops' Commission on Church Music (Church House Publishing, and Hodder and Stoughton, London, 1992), p. 275; based on: Jacqui Cooper, *Music in Parish Worship* (Central Board of Finance of the Church of England, London, [dated] 1990 [but not published until 1992]).

Less seriously, it was not made clear at this point in the text that the questionnaire covered only the newer hymnals, with the result that the press then took the statement to mean that these two books were the 'most popular' of *all* hymnals.

In other surveys, usage of *English Hymnal* in central London was found to exceed that of *Ancient and Modern*[1], while in cathedrals the major books were found to be *The New English Hymnal* 28%, *The English Hymnal* 25%, *Ancient and Modern Revised* 20%, and *Ancient and Modern New Standard* 13%.[2]

In order to obtain a genuine measure of the relative popularity of hymnals, I asked both parties to specify their levels of satisfaction with their two most-widely used books, on a scale from 1 (very satisfied) through 2 (satisfied), 3 (uncertain) and 4 (dissatisfied) to 5 (very dissatisfied). In the subsequent analysis I linked these levels of satisfaction to specific books, the average values for each book being shown in the table overleaf.

Despite its high-church overtones, *The New English Hymnal* had within a short period become the best received of all hymnals by musical directors and clergy alike. Of those using it, over nine tenths of both parties were either satisfied or very satisfied. *The English Hymnal* was, however, markedly less popular. Although more than seventeen out of twenty of both parties were either satisfied or very satisfied with *Ancient and Modern New Standard*, a few directors were very dissatisfied — I wonder why. *Ancient and Modern Revised* was somewhat more popular than *AMNS* with musical directors, but considerably less popular with the clergy. Not entirely surprisingly in view of its age, *Ancient and Modern* Standard Edition was felt to be by far the least satisfactory of the hymnals.

[1] John Winter *Music in London Churches, 1945–1982* (PhD thesis, University of East Anglia, 1984), p. 229.

[2] Berkeley Hill, *The Organisation of Music in Cathedrals in the United Kingdom* (Cathedral Organists' Association, Addington, 1989), [p. 47].

Average Levels of Satisfaction with Hymnals

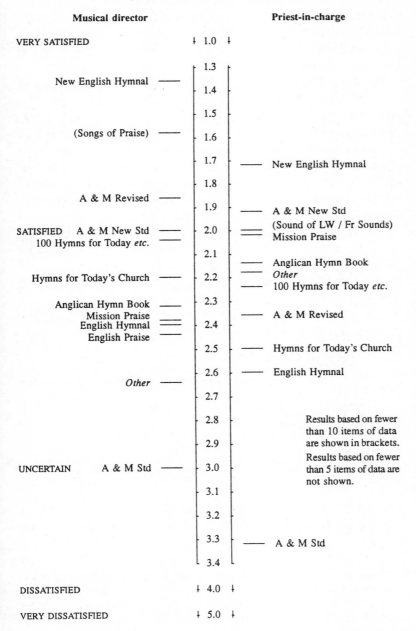

Musical director   **Priest-in-charge**

VERY SATISFIED   ⊦ 1.0 ⊦

1.3

New English Hymnal ——   1.4

1.5

(Songs of Praise) ——   1.6

1.7   —— New English Hymnal

1.8

A & M Revised ——   1.9   —— A & M New Std

SATISFIED   A & M New Std ——   2.0   ══ (Sound of LW / Fr Sounds)
100 Hymns for Today *etc.* ——   Mission Praise

2.1

2.2   —— Anglican Hymn Book
Hymns for Today's Church ——   ══ *Other*
                         —— 100 Hymns for Today *etc.*

Anglican Hymn Book ——   2.3
Mission Praise ══   —— A & M Revised
English Hymnal ══   2.4
English Praise ——

2.5   —— Hymns for Today's Church

Other ——   2.6   —— English Hymnal

2.7

2.8   Results based on fewer
                         than 10 items of data
2.9   are shown in brackets.

                         Results based on fewer
UNCERTAIN   A & M Std ——   3.0   than 5 items of data are
                         not shown.
3.1

3.2

3.3   —— A & M Std

3.4

DISSATISFIED   ⊦ 4.0 ⊦

VERY DISSATISFIED   ⊦ 5.0 ⊦

In the case of books in the 'other' category, the musical directors had the greater misgivings, over 10% being very dissatisfied. Since 'local compilation' was the largest contributor to this category, one is tempted to suppose that, at least in these cases, someone other than the musical director did the compiling.

The New English Hymnal had not become established at evangelical churches, nor had *Mission Praise* at catholic ones. Satisfaction with both *The English Hymnal* and *TNEH* increased with the level of catholicity. The same was true of *Ancient and Modern New Standard* as far as the clergy were concerned but not so for the musical directors. Another trend, but one on which both parties agreed, was that 'other' hymnals (often own compilations) were progressively more acceptable the more evangelical the church.

Despite their importance, hymns are not of course the only form of music encountered in worship. We shall now therefore proceed to examine the others. Like hymns, the psalms are usually published as complete compilations, and it is for this reason that we look next at psalters.

Psalms and Psalters

Relative usage of psalters for psalm texts[1]

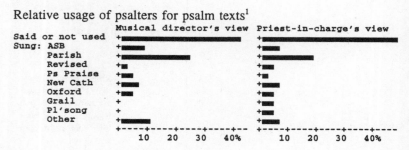

We have already reviewed (on pages 52–55) the singing of psalms. Although this practice is now much less common

---

[1] Several respondents, whilst answering other questions, left this one blank, perhaps implying that psalms are either said or not used. If so, it would increase still further the values on the first line of the chart, and reduce the others.

than in earlier years, psalms were still being sung at roughly half the services reported in the survey.

The usage of psalters was analysed in a similar way to that of hymnals, although multiple usage was found to be considerably less common. Where psalms were sung, *The Parish Psalter* was the most prevalent, followed some way behind by the *ASB Psalter*, perhaps chosen in part because of the convenience of having Rites A and B and the psalms all in the same volume. Of the remaining psalters, none was making any real headway, and indeed the two parties could not really agree on their relative usage.[1] Items in the 'other' category included responsorial psalms from *The New English Hymnal*, *Psalms for the Eucharist*, and Taizé-type settings. At one church the psalms were said over a quiet instrumental background.

In a survey of RSCM churches,[2] *The Parish Psalter* was found to be six times as widely used as the *ASB Psalter* (cf. three times now), with the *New Cathedral*, *Old Cathedral*, and *Oxford* all quite close behind the *ASB*. Only one church in 50 reported that psalms were not sung. Even allowing for differences between the two sets of churches taking part in the different surveys (RSCM churches tending to be of a conservative nature), it would appear that attitudes towards the singing of psalms have changed substantially in only a few years.

The usage of psalters in cathedrals has recently been found to be: *Oxford* 30%, *Worcester* 20%, *Revised* and *Parish* each 10%, own compilation and others 30%.[3]

Certain psalters provide music, either adjacent to the text (for example *Parish*) or as a companion volume (for

---

[1] There may have been some confusion between the *ASB Psalter* and *The Revised Psalter*. In addition, at several churches one party indicated *New Cathedral* box, while the other indicated 'other' and wrote in *Old Cathedral*. In such cases it seems likely that the *Old Cathedral* was in fact the psalter being used.

[2] Berkeley Hill, *A Survey of Church Music, 1982* (Royal School of Church Music, Addington, 1983), pp. 55, 61.

[3] Berkeley Hill, *The Organisation of Music in Cathedrals in the United Kingdom* (Cathedral Organists' Association, Addington, 1989), [p.47].

example *New Cathedral*). Other psalters provide no music, and even sometimes in the case of those that do, users take the music from another publication, and the musical directors were invited to provide information on this. However, in practice only a few did so, which implies widespread usage of the set music.[1]

Psalms, in particular those set to Anglican chants, have sometimes been criticised because of the difficulties encountered by congregations in singing them. So I asked:

If psalms are sung, who sings them?

 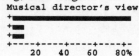 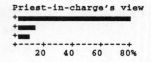

The third line of the table includes the use of responsorial psalms (two respondents indicated that the singing was alternately by congregation and cantor), but it is also not unknown for choir and congregation to sing alternate verses in a similar way to decani and cantoris in cathedral choirs. Any discrepancy between the sets of figures may simply be because the clergy describe what is supposed to happen, while the directors tell what happens in practice — in the words of one: 'sung by choir, muttered by congregation'.

Having drawn up a league table of the relative levels of acclaim of the various hymnals, I did the same for psalters. I asked both parties to specify their level of satisfaction with their most widely used psalter, on the same scale as before, namely 1 (very satisfied) through 2 (satisfied), 3 (uncertain) and 4 (dissatisfied) to 5 (very dissatisfied). The average figures for each psalter are shown on the table overleaf.

---

[1] Six churches had compiled their own set of chants, while a further three were each using more than one published book. The number of churches reported to be using specific chant books was as follows: *Anglican* 6, *Old Cathedral* 5, *RSCM* and *Parish* each 4, *New Cathedral* 2, and four other books each being used at only one church. One of these was *A Manual of Plainsong*, and it seems likely that this volume, although not reported as such, was in use at most if not all of the churches using plainsong.

Average Levels of Satisfaction with Psalters

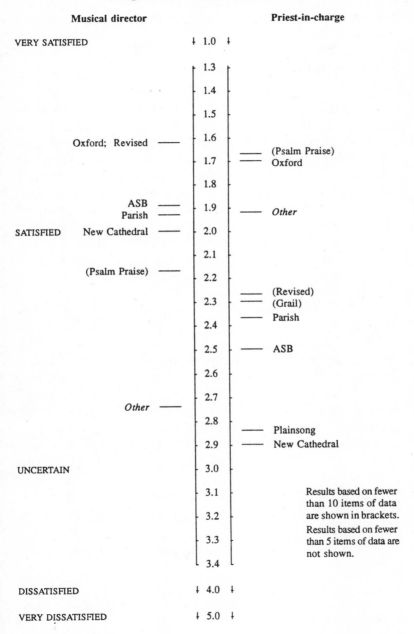

There was a wide range of views on the suitability of the various psalters used. The only book to be rated highly by both parties, albeit within a very select group, was the *Oxford Psalter*.

Settings of the Eucharist and Canticles

If there is any music at all at a service, it will almost certainly take the form of hymns. If slightly more elaborate music is included, it will probably take the form of a setting of certain parts of the eucharistic liturgy (usually the Kyries and/or Gloria, Sanctus, Benedictus, and Agnus Dei), or the canticles at Morning or Evening Prayer. In three quarters of the services they were sung (in Latin at one service in 60).

A total of 79 churches specified their eucharistic settings. These were, in decreasing order of usage: Merbecke, Richard Shephard *Addington* or *Wiltshire*, Dom Gregory Murray *People's Mass*, Patrick Appleford *New English Mass*, Martin Shaw *Folk Mass*, Ian Hubbard (either his own or the *Salisbury* setting composed jointly with Neil Cocking), John Rutter, local composition, *Darke in F*, plus some thirty other settings. One of the churches using Merbecke was doing so in a Rite A service — it is unclear whether the words had been changed to the Rite A version. Dakers, in particular, regards such manipulation of the text as a poor compromise[1], whilst a similar adaptation of Shaw's *Folk Mass* was withdrawn at the request of the composer's widow.[2] In a survey[3] of music sung at services in British cathedrals during 1986, *Darke in F* was first among the communion services, Merbecke 13th, and *Addington* 48th=.

Twelve churches were, at least occasionally, singing the evening canticles to a setting. These included, in decreasing

---

[1] Lionel Dakers, *Church Music in a Changing World* (Mowbray, Oxford, 1984), p. 55.

[2] John Winter, *Music in London Churches, 1945–1982* (PhD thesis, University of East Anglia, 1984), p. 87.

[3] John Patton, *Survey of Music and Repertoire* (Friends of Cathedral Music, Chichester, 1990), [pp. 3–7].

order, *Stanford in B flat*, *Stanford in C*, and *Noble in B minor*. At cathedrals, *Stanford in C* was first among the evening canticles, *Noble in B minor* third, and *Stanford in B flat* fourth. Three churches were, at least occasionally, singing the morning canticles to a setting. At all three, *Stanford in B flat* was one of the services sung. At cathedrals, it was top of the morning canticles.

Anthems

Most of the music that we have considered so far has, at least in theory, been open to everyone to sing. The same cannot be said of the remaining music found in services, and this can give rise to mixed feelings.

> It is not uncommon to find the singing of an anthem which rings more of 'performance' than prayerfulness, as the people sit back after the 'act' has been announced to enjoy (or endure) the result. Anthems should bring us to our knees, but this is not always so. . . .
>
> The principle of including words of a former age in a modern rite is well established through the use of anthems. Well-chosen and properly performed, these neither interrupt the flow nor intrude into the service and can be a powerful means of proclaiming the Faith.[1]

But just how frequently *are* anthems sung nowadays?

Frequency of anthems

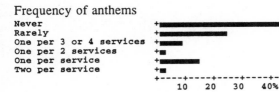

[1] *In Tune With Heaven*, Report of The Archbishops' Commission on Church Music (Church House Publishing, and Hodder and Stoughton, London, 1992), pp. 42, 184.

At almost half the services an anthem was never sung, whilst at a further quarter one was performed only 'rarely'.[1] Overall, therefore, an anthem cannot be regarded as a common event. One director added the comment 'alas' to his tick in the first category.

An earlier question (page 147) asked whether the service was 'never', 'sometimes' or 'always/nearly always' attended by a choir. When I re-analysed the frequency of anthems using only those cases where the choir was 'sometimes' present, I was surprised to find that an anthem was never sung in almost half the cases. Presumably the function of such choirs is merely to lead the congregational singing, but why they should do this at some times and not others is unclear. Possibly their level of commitment is such that they can function only at the major festivals. Finally, I analysed the frequency of anthems using only those cases where the choir was 'always/nearly always' present. Here I was equally surprised to find that one in seven of the responses indicated that an anthem was 'never' sung, and one in three only 'rarely'. Such a scarcity of anthems suggests either that the choir is incapable of singing them (in which case its ability to lead the congregational singing must also be in some doubt), or begs the question of whether the choir ought perhaps to be used more fully.

I asked directors to specify up to three typical anthems sung by the choir. The following table shows the thirteen most-cited anthems and, for comparison, the number of times that each was performed in British cathedrals in 1986,

---

[1] In the ACCMUS statistical report (Jacqui Cooper, *Music in Parish Worship* (London, [dated] 1990 [but not published until 1992]), p.54), the question: 'Does your church's musical repertoire include Choir/singing group anthems?' evoked a 54% 'yes' response, which implies 46% 'no'. This corresponds closely to my 47% 'never' response above. The picture painted by the Commission (page 275 of *In Tune With Heaven*) that 'over 50% [of churches included in their repertoire] . . . choir/singing group anthems', though true, is incomplete.

and its position in the order of the 250 most-performed anthems.[1]

RELATIVE FREQUENCIES OF PERFORMANCE
OF THE MOST COMMON ANTHEMS

		This survey		Cathedrals	
		No. of times		No. of times	
Composer	Title	cited	Pos.	sung	Pos.
S.S. Wesley	Lead me, Lord	14	1st	57	61st=
W.A. Mozart	Ave verum	* 10	2nd	138	4th=
Edward Elgar	Ave verum	8	3rd	101	17th
S.S. Wesley	Blessed be the God	6	4th	103	16th
William Byrd	Ave verum	5	5th=	145	2nd=
Maurice Greene	Thou visitest the earth	5	5th=	42	98th=
John Stainer	God so loved the world	5	5th=	31	139th=
J.S. Bach	Jesu, joy	4	8th	69	44th
Thomas Attwood	Come, Holy Ghost	3	9th=	43	94th=
Adrian Batten	O, sing joyfully	3	9th=	66	45th=
William Harris	Behold, the tabernacle	3	9th=	18	234th=
John Goss	O, Saviour of the world	3	9th=	23	187th=
Charles Wood	O thou the central orb	3	9th=	108	12th

* Nine in Latin, one in English

It is reassuring that all the most-cited anthems in the present survey find their way onto cathedral music lists, although it is perhaps not surprising that there seems to be no correlation between their relative positions. Possibly less encouraging is the fact that *Lead me, Lord* appeared to be the most widespread of all. Approximately a hundred other anthems were also cited. The most-widely performed anthem in Patton's cathedral survey, Stanford's *Beati quorum via* (162 times), was cited only twice in the present survey — but then it *was* written for a six-part choir!

For each church I assessed the choir's ability according to the most difficult of the anthems cited. For example, if its most ambitious anthem was *Lead me, Lord* or Mozart's *Ave*

[1] John Patton, *Survey of Music and Repertoire* (Friends of Cathedral Music, Chichester, 1990), [pp. 7–12].

verum, this was classified as '1'. *Blessed be the God and Father*, or *O thou the central orb* were classified as '2', whilst *This is the record of John* by Orlando Gibbons, or *Faire is the heaven* by William Harris brought the choir into category '3'. The result of this classification was: three fifths in Class 1, three tenths in Class 2, and one tenth in Class 3. More than half the choirs appeared therefore to perform only music which presents scarcely any challenge either to performers or to listeners. This was not necessarily through any fault of either the musical directors or the choirs themselves, but it may well be a serious disincentive for recruiting additional members, especially those with some knowledge of music.

> It is a thing plainly repugnant to the Word of God, and the custom of the primitive Church, to have publick Prayer in the Church . . . in a tongue not understanded of the people.[1]

Attitudes change. Where anthems were sung at all in the present survey, the proportion of those using only English texts was 50%. However, when the figures were grouped according to the director's perception of the church's level of churchmanship, a pattern emerged. The proportion of those using only English at catholic churches was 39%, at churches in the centre 56% and, as might be expected, at evangelical churches higher still at 74%.

Other Vocal Music

Musical directors were invited to specify the type of music performed by Sunday school choirs and any adult singing groups or individuals. The first seemed to perform only music written for children and, although the answers tended not to be specific, the clear impression was that in general it had not come from the pen of a classical composer. Adult

---

[1] Article No. 24 of the 39 *Articles of Religion* ('agreed upon by Archbishops and Bishops of both Provinces and the whole clergy in the Convocation holden at London in the year 1562 for the avoiding of diversities of opinions and for the establishing of consent touching true religion') (London, 1562).

groups tended to be polarised in outlook within their repertoire, singing either from one of the more charismatic hymnbooks or, in a few cases, items from the traditional repertoire, but in general not both. Only one such group sang the works of both Thomas Tallis and Graham Kendrick (the two names were adjacent in the list!). At three churches the singing group sang music from Taizé. Several churches appeared to see a major function of the singing group as teaching the latest music to the congregation.

Solo singers too tended to be polarised between contemporary songs on the one hand, and classical arias on the other (*Messiah*, *Crucifixion*, and *Olivet to Calvary* receiving special mention).

A Couple of Barometers

There were two matters on which I felt that the musical director and the priest-in-charge might hold significantly different views. The first concerned the hypothetical disbanding of the choir (the question being asked only in those cases where there was indeed a choir).

If the choir disbanded, how would the standard of congregational singing alter?

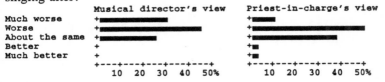

The two parties were certainly not of one mind on this matter, the clergy taking a significantly more optimistic view of the idea. Dakers takes issue with the view probably in the minds of some of them:

> We should have no illusions, nor should we be unduly influenced by the thinking which dictates that if a choir is present the congregation will not sing. The fact is that even when there is no choir there is no automatic guarantee that the congregation will sing . . . because Anglican parish church worship is conditioned to the presence of a choir. . . . The belief, however fashionable in

some quarters, that if you dispense with the choir the congregation will take on a more active musical role is not borne out by the results.[1]

The second question concerned whether the choir should do any more than merely lead the congregational singing:

In some churches, the choir sings alone for a considerable part of the service. If there is a choir, which one of the following most closely describes the situation?

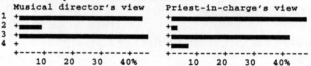

where: 1 = Choir does not sing alone and does not wish to do so;
            2 = Choir does not sing alone, but would like to do so;
            3 = Choir sings alone with general assent;
            4 = Choir sings alone, causing some resentment.

Several points emerge. Firstly, the directors and clergy agreed that the choir sang alone for a considerable part of the service in roughly 50% of cases, although their perceptions of how much constitutes 'considerable' may well have varied. Secondly, in the case where the choir did *not* sing alone, the musical directors reported that one choir in six was not entirely happy with the situation, compared with only one choir in 21 reported by the clergy. Finally, in the case where the choir *did* sing alone, the clergy reported that there was resentment amongst one congregation in eight, compared with only one congregation in 93 reported by the musical directors. The discrepancies in the figures are even greater than I anticipated, and point to a failure of clergy and musical directors to communicate — with each other, the musical director with the congregation, and the clergy with the choir.

---

[1] Lionel Dakers, *Church Music in a Changing World* (Mowbray, Oxford, 1984), pp. 89–90.

Summary

In order to bring together the varied strands of this chapter (and one or two from earlier ones also) let us imagine that we had decided to attend a service; what might we expect to find? First, it is clear that we have to choose our time very carefully in order to find a service with any music at all — less frequent than once a week in a quarter of the churches in the survey. However, we can at least be sure of a seat — at one church in six we would be most unlikely to find more than twenty people in the congregation.

We pick up our service book and hymnal. The former will probably be an *ASB* (for Rite A communion — a one-in-three chance, or Rite B — a one-in-seven) or a *BCP* (for Evening Prayer perhaps — a one-in-five chance). The most likely hymnal will be *Ancient and Modern Revised*, although *Ancient and Modern New Standard* or *The New English Hymnal* will be more likely if the church has recently obtained a new set of books. If psalms are sung at all, they will probably be taken from *The Parish Psalter*.

Our singing will almost certainly be accompanied on the organ, and there will be a 50/50 chance of it being led by a choir. Although we may be impressed by the latter's numerical strength — sixteen on average — and by the reassuringly high proportion of younger members, notably girls, we may as the service progresses become less impressed with its musical capabilities.

On our way out at the end of the service, as we return our books, we exchange a brief word with the priest. However, we find that we have missed the organist — he and the choir have left through the vestry door.

7

Happy Are They[1]

Problem Areas and Ways of
Improving the Partnership

Just how happy *are* musical directors with the pattern of musical usage in worship today? How happy are the clergy with this pattern, and how happy do they think other people — musicians and non-musicians alike — are with it?

In this chapter we examine the levels of satisfaction of both parties with various aspects of the music at their respective churches. Armed with this information, we then go on to explore some of the implications of setting up the equivalent of a 'computer-dating agency' in order to optimise the partnership between the clergy and their respective musical directors.

Sweet are the Songs[2]

I wanted to discover how satisfied the musical directors and clergy felt about the state of music in worship at the churches following the various upheavals that we looked at in Chapter 1. I therefore asked each party to indicate its level of satisfaction with the following:

---

[1] Robert Bridges from C. Coffin, [in, for example,] *Hymns Ancient and Modern Revised* (Clowes, Beccles, 1950), No. 261.
[2] Part of verse 2 of the above hymn.

- the working relationship with the other party;
- the musical director's musical competence (asked of the priest only);[1]
- the musical director's understanding of the forms of worship used (asked of the priest only);
- the priest-in-charge's understanding of the use of music in worship (asked of the musical director only);
- the musical competence of the younger members of the choir;
- the musical competence of the adult members of the choir;
- the general conduct of the younger members of the choir;
- the general attitude of the adult members of the choir;
- the main (or only) hymnal;
- the second hymnal (if applicable);
- the main (or only) psalter;[2]
- the overall use of music in the worship at services.

In addition, I asked both parties to assess the levels of satisfaction of certain other individuals or groups with the overall use of music in the worship at services. These others were:

- the priest-in-charge (asked of the musical director only);
- the musical director (asked of the priest only);
- the congregation;
- the choir (where applicable);
- a non-churchgoer who happened to be visiting the church;

---

[1] We have already noted that in those cases where the priest-in-charge and musical director were one and the same person, the results have been included only in a clergy capacity. However, a special case arises when we are asking a priest for his opinion of himself in his other capacity, for example, his own musical competence as musical director. These results too have been excluded, although admittedly in some cases they were very entertaining! The corresponding question to directors concerning the priest's theological and liturgical competence could not reasonably be asked, although the responses might have been most illuminating.

[2] The results of this and the previous two questions have already been analysed for specific books on pages 152–154 and 156–158.

- a Christian visitor with a reasonable interest in serious music;
- that same Christian visitor if he/she joined the choir (where applicable).

Several respondents suggested that there should have been a further question: 'In your view, how satisfied is God?'. Others, however, might perhaps have misconstrued it as flippant.

In each case, the scale was from 1 (very satisfied), through 2 (satisfied), 3 (uncertain) and 4 (dissatisfied) to 5 (very dissatisfied). The average figures are shown overleaf. The levels of satisfaction of the musical directors and the clergy themselves are shown in the left-hand table; their perceptions of the levels of satisfaction of others appear in the right-hand one.

Nine musical directors out of ten, and a similar proportion of priests, reported that their working relationship was satisfactory or very satisfactory: this is most encouraging. (However, a small note of caution will be sounded when we look at these figures again on page 175.) They were only slightly less happy with the other's understanding of what might be termed the grey area between their roles.

Less complimentary were their views on the musical competence of the choir, in particular the juniors. I wonder whether this is a reflection on the type of musical education provided by schools, or perhaps it is simply that those who are more talented prefer to make music elsewhere. Whatever the reason, it is far from encouraging, since today's juniors will form the core of the adult choir (or even of the adult church) of tomorrow. In between, lies the more subjective question concerning the juniors' conduct. Quite possibly some musical directors interpreted it in terms of musical conduct, whilst the clergy considered it in a wider religious context. Directors may well be anxious not to lose 'the adult choir of tomorrow', and feel obliged to be correspondingly tolerant.

Average Levels of Own Satisfaction

Musical director		Priest-in-charge

VERY SATISFIED   ǂ 1.0 ǂ

```
                                   ┌ 1.6 ┐
Working relationship with PC  ───  │     │  ───  Working relationship with MD
                                   │ 1.7 │
Adult choir's attitude  ____       │     │
PC's understanding of use of       │ 1.8 │  ───  MD's musical competence
      music in worship  ____       │     │  ───  MD's understanding of forms
Young choir's conduct   ────       │     │       of worship
                                   │ 1.9 │
SATISFIED                          │ 2.0 │  ───  Adult choir's attitude
                                   │     │  ───  Young choir's conduct
Main psalter  ____                 │ 2.1 │
Main hymnal   ────                 │     │
2nd hymnal    ────                 │     │
                                   │ 2.2 │  ───  Adult choir's musical
Adult choir's musical              │     │       competence
         competence  ____          │ 2.3 │  ───  Main and 2nd hymnals
             Overall ────          │     │
                                   │ 2.4 │  ───  Main psalter
Young choir's musical  ____        │     │       Overall
        competence                 │ 2.5 │  ───  Young choir's musical
                                   │     │       competence
                                   │ 2.6 │
                                   │ 2.7 │
                                   │ 2.8 │
                                   │ 2.9 │
UNCERTAIN                          └ 3.0 ┘
```

DISSATISFIED   ǂ 4.0 ǂ

VERY DISSATISFIED   ǂ 5.0 ǂ

Average Perceptions of Overall Levels of Satisfaction of Others

Musical Director		**Priest-in-charge**

VERY SATISFIED   ┤ 1.0 ┤

                                        ┬ 1.6 ┬

                                        ─ 1.7 ─

                                        ─ 1.8 ─

                                        ─ 1.9 ─

SATISFIED   2.0

Priest-in-charge ——   2.1

Choir ══
Congregation   2.2   —— Congregation

                                        2.3   —— Choir

Christian with interest in serious
music in choir ——   2.4   —— Musical director
Non-churchgoer ——

                                        2.5

Christian with interest in serious   2.6
music ——

                                        2.7   —— Non-churchgoer
                                                  ══ Christian with interest in
                                        2.8   serious music in choir

                                        2.9

                                                  —— Christian with interest in
UNCERTAIN   ┴ 3.0 ┴   serious music

DISSATISFIED   ┤ 4.0 ┤

VERY DISSATISFIED   ┤ 5.0 ┤

Although four out of five of both parties were satisfied or very satisfied with the attitude of the adult members of the choir, as many as one in twelve expressed dissatisfaction or worse. The nature of this may well be different in the two cases (differing views, for example, on the relative seriousness of missing choir practice and talking during the sermon). One priest regretted the unwillingness of the adults to assist in the training of the younger members of the choir.

Musical directors and clergy were less than satisfied in a significant proportion of cases (more than a quarter and more than a third respectively) with the overall use of music in worship at their church. When they were asked to assess each other's level of satisfaction, the musical directors were rather over-optimistic (2.09, as opposed to the real clergy value of 2.47). However, the clergy were much more accurate in their assessment (2.39, comparable to the real directors' value of 2.31). The directors' perception of the congregation's level of satisfaction was a little more optimistic than the clergy's perception, although one director suggested that the congregation's state of satisfaction was more strictly one of apathy. However impracticable, it would have been interesting to learn the actual views of the congregations.

Neither musical directors nor clergy rated the level of satisfaction of a non-churchgoer very highly, namely 2.46 and 2.73 respectively. Even more pessimistic were the views expressed concerning the lot of a musical Christian visitor. Half the musical directors, and almost two thirds of the clergy, were not confident that such a person would feel satisfied. His/her position would seem to be but little improved if he/she were to join the choir — if indeed there was a choir at the church in question. One in six of the clergy felt that such a person would be dissatisfied or very dissatisfied, whilst only one in ten of the musical directors felt that their new chorister would be very satisfied. Again it would be interesting to know the reasons for such pessimism, especially among the clergy, and the extent to which this was perceived to be a serious problem.

By a wide margin therefore, in the view of both parties, those least likely to be satisfied with the role played by music are the non-churchgoing visitor and the Christian visitor with an interest in serious music, whether or not the latter joined the choir. It may reasonably be inferred that a non-Christian musical visitor would be equally dissatisfied. For whatever reasons, both parties perceived the levels of satisfaction of both the existing congregation and the existing choir to be much higher. If the Christian Church exists for those outside it, as has been periodically advocated, then on the musical front at least, the churches taking part in the survey seem to be fighting a losing battle (and there is no reason to suppose that the situation is significantly better elsewhere). Furthermore, if the Christian musical visitor is frustrated by the music as it currently exists, there is surely a risk that he/she will not wish to become involved, thus exacerbating the situation.

I also examined the levels of satisfaction in terms of churchmanship, only to find that in general the figures were remarkably consistent. One exception was that although an amateur musician would be more satisfied in the choir of a catholic or middle-of-the-road church than in the congregation, this would not be the case in an evangelical church.

So where do we go from here? Is there anything that can be done to improve the situation?

The Perfect Match

The secret of a successful computer-dating agency lies, so I am led to believe, in its ability to pair together two people whose various characteristics are complementary.[1] In principle this sounded straightforward enough, so I wondered whether it might be possible to launch a similar scheme enabling musical directors to find that 'extra-special' priest, or the clergy to find the musical director of their

---

[1] For a good match, the agency will need large numbers of clients on its database, and it is of course preferable that they be unattached. I gather, however, some agencies are more conscientious over these points than others!

dreams. Details of the mathematics[1] are outside the scope of this book, but some of the early results in this field are very illuminating. Let us look at some of them.

The clergy and the musical directors had both been asked, on a scale from 1 to 5 (page 168), how satisfied they were with their working relationship with the other party. As a first step, for each party I ran a series of 'correlation tests', to see whether that party's level of satisfaction could be statistically related to any of the other 'variables' that had been under scrutiny in the questionnaire. An initial revelation was the fact that each party felt the relationship to be more satisfactory where the other party was younger than him/her. Similarly, each party preferred to have been in post longer than the other. If the musical director felt that it was in general advantageous for a director to co-operate in a flexible way, then he/she was more likely to be satisfied with the working relationship with the priest. On the other hand, if the priest felt it to be advantageous, then the musical director was less likely to be satisfied. As Professor Joad would have said: 'It all depends what you mean by *flexible*'.

If a priest felt that a musical director's ability as a solo organist was an advantage, then this boded well in the priest's eyes for a satisfactory working relationship. If, however, the musical director felt it to be advantageous, then this pointed (again from the priest's point of view) to an unsatisfactory working relationship. If a musical director was involved with other church-music interests outside his/her own church, the priest was likely to find the relationship easier. Again, in the priest's eyes, a satisfactory relationship was associated with much time spent in discussion. However, we must be cautious here. If a priest finds a relationship with a director difficult, is their failure to hold meetings a cause of this difficulty — or an effect?

[1] R.L.D. Rees, *The Role of Music and Musicians in Current English Parish Church Worship: The Attitudes of Clergy and Organists* (PhD thesis, University of Sheffield, 1991), pp. 321–337.

Other correlations which might have been anticipated were not found to be significant (or, as might be said, they were 'not proven'). These included: *(a)* the musical director's view of how advantageous it is for a director to be a practising Christian (one might have expected that a director who felt that it does not matter would get on worse with a priest than one who felt that it does); *(b)* the number of years that the priest had spent in secular employment prior to ministerial training (one might have expected that someone who had spent longer in the 'real world' might be more tolerant than someone who had not); and *(c)* the number of parties to whom a musical director should have the right of appeal in the event of dispute with the priest (someone allowing appeal to a wider court might be expected to be more tolerant).

Although these correlations give us new insights, they do not particularly help us with our 'computer-dating' project. Since any relationship is ultimately a two-way process, it may be argued that a truer view of each relationship may be obtained by combining the views of the two parties rather than looking at each in isolation. Before developing this, I had in any case been wondering the extent to which (at a given church) the parties took differing views on the state of their relationship. As might be expected, at most churches both parties held a common view, although naturally there were minor differences of perception (for example a priest being very satisfied and a director merely satisfied). However, there were instances of the director being satisfied and the priest dissatisfied or, more remarkable, the priest being very satisfied and the director being dissatisfied or (stranger still) very dissatisfied. Such situations point to one party's unwillingness to admit that there is a problem, or a failure of the parties to communicate effectively with each other or even, as a specific example of this, a differing perception of what constitutes a satisfactory working relationship. A priest might regard as ideal a relationship of total subservience on the part of the musical director!

In the circumstances I decided not to put complete faith for my 'dating' project in the two parties' stated perceptions of their working relationship. I had other possible pointers to the state of affairs (e.g. how satisfied each party was with the use of music in the worship at services), so I could build up a more complete picture of the overall level of musical satisfaction of the two parties. For each church, I defined a 'Satisfaction Index', by summing the following individual levels of satisfaction:

- director's view of priest's understanding of use of music in worship;
- director's view of working relationship with priest;
- priest's view of director's musical competence;
- priest's view of director's understanding of the forms of worship used;
- priest's view of working relationship with director;
- director's overall view of use of music in the worship at the services;
- priest's overall view of use of music in the worship at the services.

The items comprising the Satisfaction Index are not entirely arbitrary: they are the ones most closely affecting the priest and musical director. (The views of the choir, congregation, etc. are all of interest, and merit further investigation at some stage, but they do not *directly* affect the priest and the musical director.)

I then ran further correlation tests, this time against the Satisfaction Index. Further revelations were in store. In particular, an increase in any of the following was associated with an improvement in the Satisfaction Index:

- time spent in discussion between the two parties;
- the number of qualifications (not necessarily musical) held by the musical director;
- the closeness of the two parties' personal preferences on catholic/evangelical worship;
- the number of church-music associations to which the musical director belonged;

• the level of musical attainment of the priest.

Clergy may find it helpful to consider some of these points when next they are interviewing a prospective musical director.

Clearly the whole topic of levels of satisfaction defies precise quantification. No doubt there are other factors systematically affecting it, some being complex combinations of variables in the questionnaire, some not asked at all (for example, the distance that the musical director has to travel to church?). Over and above the systematic factors will be the traits of human unpredictability. That having been said, *any* attempt at systematically matching priest and musical director is surely better than no attempt at all.

I am convinced that further statistical analysis will bring to light additional predictors of the state of the relationship between the musical director and the priest. Then, if a church receives more than one application for the post of musical director, an objective test will be available to determine which of the candidates is likely to be the most suitable for the specific situation. Of course the crucial word is 'if', but I believe that yesterday's poor clergy/organist relationships are in no small measure responsible for today's dearth of organists. Have we found a means of breaking what is often seen as a vicious circle?

Conclusion

The liturgical and hymnological upheavals of the sixties, seventies and early eighties had, by the mid-eighties, left many church musicians in a state of shock. Relationships with clergy — never renowned for their warmth — appeared to be worsening. It was in this context that I embarked on a survey of the attitudes of clergy and musical directors to the role of music in current parish church worship. This book is the outcome of that survey.

Although much of the book has been devoted to the results of a questionnaire survey, the questions within in it had first to be placed in their historical and contemporary context. For this reason, I devoted the Introduction and Chapter 1 to such diverse matters as the Church of England's use of music in worship over the centuries, areas of conflict in church music, the scope of other church-music surveys, the effects of liturgical and hymnological change, and the training courses on the use of music in worship. As an introduction to my own survey, I included three case studies demonstrating problems that can arise when clergy and church musicians are in conflict.

The questionnaires themselves, distributed to the priest-in-charge and musical director (organist) at almost half the churches in a large diocese, have provided a composite picture firstly of respondents' personal backgrounds and general attitudes, and secondly, respondents' perceptions of the situation at their church, and of each other. The overall response rate to the questionnaires was over 74%. This, combined with the fact that the diocese has been shown to be a typical one, suggests that any conclusions drawn from the survey may be applied to the Church of England as a whole.

Perhaps the most depressing finding of my survey was that there appeared to be little common ground between clergy and musical directors. The clergy had little knowledge of, or ability in, music (the same can perhaps be said of some of the directors), whilst the directors' knowledge of theology was very limited. Moreover, there seemed to be little desire to develop this common ground, with little interest in either church-related musical associations or discussion groups. Added to this, neither party placed much value on a formal qualification in church music. Especially noteworthy, however, was the dissatisfaction expressed by clergy at the quantity and/or quality of their music training at theological college. The extent to which this perceived inadequacy is causing major problems in parish-church music is unclear. However, a full survey of the music training programmes of theological colleges would seem to be a worthwhile future project. Indeed, reference to no more than the present data and Crockford's[1] would enable a comparison of levels of satisfaction between different colleges to be compiled.

At the time of the survey, alarmingly little time and money were being spent on developing the churches' musical resources. For example, a typical annual music budget per member of the electoral roll was less than 20 pence. In over a third of the churches the total time spent per year in discussion between the priest-in-charge and the musical director was an hour or less (responses elsewhere in the questionnaires provided additional evidence of the two parties' failure to communicate with each other). At only

[1] *Crockford's Clerical Directory* (89th edn), (Church House Publishing, London, 1985).

one church in three was the musical director a member of the PCC; at only one in four churches was there a working group for worship, and at only one in ten a working group for music. Also somewhat alarming was the fact that at only one church in six was there more than one suitable candidate when the present musical director was appointed. However, there is hope that the seeds sown in 'National Learn the Organ Year' will in due course yield the required harvest.

The shock waves of the 'hymn explosion' have reached many churches, with *Hymns Ancient and Modern New Standard*, *The New English Hymnal* and many other compilations taking their places in the pews. Psalms, on the other hand, are not widely sung in today's parish churches.

Apart from all-male choirs (where numbers are declining, as are the numbers of boys in all choirs), membership of choirs seems to have been maintained in the most recent three-year period. This says much for the choirs' forbearance, as S.S. Wesley's *Lead me, Lord* was the anthem most commonly cited.

Both the clergy and the musical directors seemed to agree that an interest in serious music was something of an impediment to a worshipper in many of today's services. If true, and I believe it is, this is a serious matter. Admittedly thirty years ago, the Church of England may have had too much of a middle-class approach to its worship and music. Now the musical pendulum seems in danger of swinging too far in the opposite direction. Music should be an aid to worship, not an impediment to it, and every effort must be made for this to apply to all. It is, however, a fact of life that people's musical tastes differ (even BBC Radios 1, 2 and 3 can barely cover the spectrum), and finding a solution to this in the church environment is not easy:

> The relationship between music, Christian worship and culture is very complex. . . . I suspect it is something with which we shall always be struggling, because what is culturally meaningful and acceptable to one person is anathema to another.[1]

---

[1] Alan Reeve, 'One Man's Meat' in *Christian Music* (Summer 1990), p. 18.

The comment of a former Poet Laureate is no less relevant eighty years later:

> It seems to me that the clergy are responsible. If they say that the hymns (words and music) which keep me away from the church door draw others thither and excite useful religious emotions . . . all I can urge is that they should have at least *one* service a week where people like myself can attend without being moved to laughter.[1]

Finding the right balance for a particular church between traditional and non-traditional music is a very sensitive matter, requiring considerable discussion between the priest and musical director, and preferably other parties as well.

One Incumbent stressed the importance of treating *all* styles of music seriously, so that modern choruses are sung *well* and not treated lightheartedly. In this way he had found new material was acceptable to most people.[2]

By a strange coincidence, two somewhat similar projects, namely my own and that of the Archbishops' Commission, were independently initiated within two years of each other. I respect and at the same time regret the Commission's decision that, for reasons of confidentiality, the two projects had to remain independent of one another.

Both surveys do, however, agree that parish church music is not in a particularly healthy state. However, despite this gloom there are one or two rays of hope. Firstly, the unusually high response rate from both the clergy and musical directors to my questionnaires implies a measure of concern. This can perhaps be seen as encouraging in the longer term: a problem cannot be resolved until it is perceived to be a problem. Secondly, I have suggested in Chapter 7 ways of predicting how 'successful' a musical

---

[1] R. Bridges, 'About hymns' in *Church Music Society Occasional Papers*, 2, (1911); quoted by Nicholas Temperley, *The Music of the English Church* (CUP, Cambridge, 1979), p. 321.

[2] *A Joyful Noise* (Resource Paper 84:7) (Administry, St. Albans, 1984), p.3.

director will be in a particular church with a given priest. This will perhaps encourage priests to think more deeply when appointing a new musical director. In fact, one of the priests taking part in the survey reported that he had found the questionnaire most helpful when interviewing applicants. Clergy and musical directors may even be persuaded that it would be in the best interests of both parties to spend more time in discussion with one another. The absence of adequate discussion was a factor common to all three of the case studies. However, the work so far undertaken on matching clergy and musical directors is only a first step, and many more interesting correlations undoubtedly lie beneath the surface of the data, merely waiting to be trawled.

In response to a report of my project[1], I received a poem[2] which provides a fitting epilogue. Not only does the poem confirm at least two of my findings, but it also implies the need for a further project, namely a survey of congregational tastes in church music.

---

[1] 'Role Conflict' in *Church Times*, 6461 (12 December 1986), p. 8.
[2] This poem by H. Ford Benson is believed to have appeared in a Baptist publication c. 1920. It is a pastiche of a poem by Lewis Carroll in *Through the Looking Glass*.

The Parson and the Organist

The Parson and the Organist
  Were walking side by side,
Said the Parson to the Organist,
  'Your tunes I can't abide'.

'I'm sorry', said the latter,
  'That our tastes should disagree,
But I really must say frankly
  That your sermons don't touch *me*'.

And so they fell discussing
  From their different points of view,
The pulpit and the organ-loft,
  But quite forgot *the pew*.

Till up came a churchwarden,
  Who was passing by that way,
And hearing the discussion
  He just thought he'd have his say.

'Look here,' said he, 'my brothers,
  You both are in the wrong!
One shows the way to heaven
  And the other leads the song.

'Let each to his vocation
  His best endeavours bring,
For when we get to Heaven
  We must all know how to sing.'

This ended the discussion,
  For they felt that he was right,
So the Parson and the Organist
  Shook hands and said 'Good-night'.

———————

To this I can only add 'Amen'.

Advent Sunday 1992

Appendix

List of Addresses

CHIME
1 Lioncroft Cottages, Upwood Road, Bury, Huntingdon, Cambs., PE17 1PA.

Christian Copyright Licensing
PO Box 1339, Eastbourne, East Sussex, BN21 4YF.

Christian Musicians' and Artists' Trust
PO Box 45, Patchway, Bristol, BS12 6RT.

Colchester Institute
Sheepen Road, Colchester, Essex, CO3 3LL.

Faculty of Church Music
St Jude's Rectory, 49 Upper Tooting Park, London, SW17 7SN.

Guild of Church Musicians
'Hillbrow', Godstone Road, Bletchingley, Surrey, RH1 4PY.

Incorporated Association of Organists
18 Duffins Close, Shawclough, Rochdale, Lancashire, OL12 6XA.

Music and Worship Foundation
151 Bath Road, Hounslow, Middlesex, TW3 3BU.

Pratt Green Trust
191 Creighton Avenue, Finchley, London N2 9BN.

Royal Academy of Music, Marylebone Road, London, NW1 5HT.

Royal College of Organists
7 St Andrew's Street, Holborn, London, EC4A 3LQ.

Royal School of Church Music
Addington Palace, Croydon, CR9 5AD.

University of East Anglia
Norwich, NR4 7TJ.

Bibliography

The Alternative Service Book 1980 (Clowes, SPCK, CUP, OUP, Mowbray, and Hodder and Stoughton, London, 1980).

The Alternative Service Book 1980 (An annotated list of music published by the RSCM and others for: Communion Rite A, Communion Rite B, Canticles, etc.) (Royal School of Church Music, Addington, 1988).

Church Statistics: Some facts and figures about the Church of England (Central Board of Finance of the Church of England, London, 1989).

Jacqui Cooper, *Music in Parish Worship* (Central Board of Finance of the Church of England, London, [dated] 1990 [but not published until 1992]).

Copyright and the Local Church, (Pratt Green Trust, London, 1989).

Crockford's Clerical Directory (89th edn) (Church House Publishing, London, 1985).

Lionel Dakers:

— *Church Music at the Crossroads* (Marshall, Morgan and Scott, London, 1970).

— *A Handbook of Parish Music* (Mowbray, London, 1976).

— *Church Music in a Changing World* (Mowbray, Oxford, 1984).

— *Choosing and Using Hymns* (Mowbray, London, 1985).

Stephen Dean, 'Roman Catholic Music: the Recent Past and the Future' in *In Spirit and in Truth* (ed. Robin Sheldon) (Hodder and Stoughton, London, 1989), pp. 31–48.

Leslie J. Francis, *Rural Anglicanism* (Collins, London, 1985).

Berkeley Hill:
— *A Survey of Church Music, 1982* (Royal School of Church Music, Addington, 1983).
— *The Organisation of Music in Cathedrals in the United Kingdom* (Cathedral Organists' Association, Addington, 1989).

Roger Homan and David Martin, *Theological Colleges and the Book of Common Prayer: a Survey* (Prayer Book Society, London, 1986).

Christopher Idle, *Hymns in Today's Language* (Booklet No. 81) (Grove, Nottingham, 1982).

In Tune With Heaven, Report of the Archbishops' Commission on Church Music (Church House Publishing, and Hodder and Stoughton, London, 1992).

R.C.D. Jasper and Paul F. Bradshaw, *A Companion to the Alternative Service Book* (SPCK, London, 1986).

A Joyful Noise (Resource Paper 84:7) (Administry, St. Albans, 1984).

John Leach, *Liturgy and Liberty* (MARC, Eastbourne, 1989).

Robin Leaver, *A Hymn Book Survey 1962–80* (Booklet No. 71) (Grove, Nottingham, 1980).

Robin Leaver, David Mann and David Parkes, *Ways of Singing the Psalms* (Collins, London, 1985).

Kenneth R. Long, *The Music of the English Church* (Hodder and Stoughton, London, 1972).

David R. Moores, 'Clergy-Organist Relationships' in *The American Organist*, August 1985, pp. 46–47.

Music in Church, Report of the Committee appointed in 1948 by the Archbishops of Canterbury and York (Church Information Board, Westminster, 1951); revised edition (CIB, Westminster, 1957).

Music in Worship, Report of the Archbishops' Committee appointed in May 1922, (Central Board of Finance and SPCK, London, 1922); revised edition (Press and Publications Board of the Church Assembly, London, 1932).

Organists' Guide to Employment, (Incorporated Society of Musicians) (London, 1990).

Oxford Diocesan Year Book, 1988 (Oxford Diocesan Board of Finance, Oxford, 1987).

John Patton, *Survey of Music and Repertoire* (Friends of Cathedral Music, Chichester, 1990).

Michael Perry, *Psalm Praise Worship Index* (Falcon, London, 1977).

Robin L.D. Rees, *The Role of Music and Musicians in Current English Parish Church Worship: The Attitudes of Clergy and Organists* (PhD thesis, University of Sheffield, 1991).

Robin L.D. Rees and Leslie J. Francis, 'Clergy Response Rates to Work-Related Questionnaires: A Relationship Between Age, Work Load and Burnout?', *Social Behavior and Personality 19*, No. 1 (1991) pp. 45–51.

Robin Sheldon (ed.), *In Spirit and in Truth* (Hodder and Stoughton, London, 1989).

Nicholas Temperley, *The Music of the English Parish Church* (CUP, Cambridge, 1979).

John Winter, *Music in London Churches, 1945–1982* (PhD thesis, University of East Anglia, 1984).